LA

LOST&FOUND

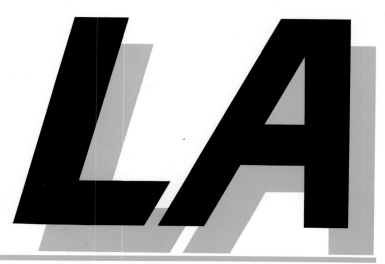

LA
LOST&FOUND

AN ARCHITECTURAL HISTORY OF LOS ANGELES

SAM HALL KAPLAN

PRINCIPAL PHOTOGRAPHER
JULIUS SHULMAN

BOOK DESIGNER
DANA LEVY
PERPETUA PRESS

CROWN PUBLISHERS, INC.
New York

CONTENTS

For Peggy and Josef, my L.A. companions

Photo credits and permissions appear on page 224.

Published by Crown Publishers, Inc., 225 Park Avenue South, New York, New York 10003 and represented in Canada by the Canadian MANDA Group.

CROWN is a trademark of Crown Publishers, Inc.

Manufactured in Japan

Library of Congress Cataloging-in-Publication Data

Kaplan, Sam Hall.
    L.A. lost and found.

    Bibliography: p.
    1. Architecture—California—Los Angeles.
2. Los Angeles (Calif.)—Buildings, structures, etc.
I. Title. II Title: LA lost and found.
NA735.L55K3 1987   720'.9794'94   86-13526
ISBN 0-517-56184-0

10 9 8 7 6 5 4 3 2 1

First Edition

INTRODUCTION

Los Angeles to me has always been a curiosity: a distinctly American creation, cultivated by a rare sense of freedom and fashioned out of a desert on the edge of an ocean to become a fragmented collection of paradoxical communities and individualistic life-styles, desired and despised; second in population to the New York metropolitan area and expected to pass it by the year 2000; once the destination of the greatest migration in history and now the nation's prime port of entry for new immigrants; not a melting pot or stew but, given the climate, more a gazpacho of people and ideas. Exciting.

With its benign climate of only a little rain and a hint of seasons, its scant indigenous plant life, and its distance far from any natural resources or other metropolitan areas that could have generated symbiotic industry, Los Angeles has defied logic with the promise of new beginnings. It is "the city of the second chance," the most twentieth-century city in America. It was not accidental that the automobile culture, the movie and aerospace industries, and Disneyland took root in Los Angeles, or that almost every conceivable— and a few inconceivable—fads, fashions, and styles have at some time or other sprouted in its consenting climate and spirit.

Whether out of envy or confusion, Los Angeles has been called the earth's first experimental space colony, as well as, among other things, the new Eden, the new Jerusalem, and the new Babylon. Also Lotus Land, Lala land, autopia, and simply a mistake. Like a good straight man in a burlesque routine, Los Angeles has had more flip insults directed at it over the years than most cities. But it has also

been known as a warm and sunny, exotic land of opportunity, where one could pursue the American dream of the good life, unhampered by confining social traditions and the need for overcoats and galoshes. Certainly the stuff to stir curiosity.

It was this curiosity that prompted me in 1978 to join the *Los Angeles Times.* I saw my employment there as a writer as a sort of an urban affairs fellowship to provide me with time, a perspective, and an entrée to study the forces shaping and misshaping the phenomena of Southern California, while enjoying its hospitality and climate. My perspective until then had been limited to a few visits, books, and, of course, the movies. It was in the dark of theaters that I formed my first images of Los Angeles.

Films like *The Big Sleep, Double Indemnity, Sunset Boulevard* and, later, *Chinatown* presented the city as a place of strange mansions, sordid hotels, slick nightclubs, seedy bars, and shabby motels in which tough, honest, timeworn detectives and other rough-hewn heroes confronted criminals, conmen, and the corrupted on behalf of conflicted, often conniving, women or simply in quest of the truth. In the shadows there always seemed to be mysterious and morbid characters. For an area blessed with sunshine, there were a lot of shadows. And tragedy.

This was confirmed by books like *Miss Lonelyhearts* and *Day of the Locust,* by Nathanael West, and *The Long Goodbye* by Raymond Chandler. Later there were *True Confessions* by John Gregory Dunne and *Zoot Suit Murders* by Thomas Sanchez. They projected an image of Los Angeles as a city of disillusionment and destruction. Chandler's Philip Marlowe in *The Long Goodbye* took it all in with a gulp and glimpse: "When I got home I mixed a stiff one and stood by the open window in the living room and sipped it and listened to the groundswell of the traffic on Laurel Canyon Boulevard and looked at the glare of the big angry city hanging over the shoulder of the hills through which the boulevard had been cut . . . A city no worse than others, a city rich and vigorous and full of pride, a city lost and beaten and full of emptiness."

But also in that city, careening from curb to curb, racing over cliffs, hanging from rooftops and bending clock hands high above the streets, were Charlie Chaplin, Harold Lloyd, Buster Keaton, Laurel and Hardy, the Marx Brothers and a host of frantic comics, racing across the screen to make me laugh.

When I became involved in planning and architecture, I learned that L.A. was also the city where the Arts and Crafts movement bloomed in the ultimate bungalow, the "California" bungalow, fashioned by Charles and Henry Greene; where the Art Deco style came to full flower; and where Irving Gill, Frank Lloyd Wright, R. M. Schindler, Richard Neutra, Cliff May, Henry Dreyfuss, Charles and Ray Eames, Walt Disney, and a host of other designers, each in his own way, championed concepts that in time changed the shape of America.

Yet there was Jeremy Pordage, in *After Many a Summer Dies the Swan* by Aldous Huxley, viewing Los Angeles for the first time: "Primitive Methodist churches built, surprisingly enough, in the style of the Cartuja at Granada, Catholic churches like Canterbury Cathedral, synagogues disguised as Hagia Sophia, Christian Science churches with pillars and pediments like banks," and "facades of houses, all new, almost all in good taste—elegant and witty pastiches of Lutyens manor houses, of Little Trianons, of Monticellos; lighthearted parodies of Le Corbusier's solemn machine-for-living; fantastic adaptations of Mexican haciendas and New England farms . . . The houses succeeded one another, like the pavilions at some endless international exhibition. Gloucestershire followed Andalusia and gave place in turn to Touraine and Oaxaca, Dusseldorf and Massachusetts."

In more portentous tones, fellow urban planners, architecture critics, and visiting experts condemned Los Angeles as a chaotic collection of suburbs, a sprawling abstraction which alienated its residents and destroyed the environment, while corrupting the rest of the country with flimsy fantasies. The contradictions overflowed.

When visiting Los Angeles I found, as I had suspected, that it was more than an autopolis, an amorphous mass of housing tracts and shopping centers held together by a mesh of crowded freeways, or some back lot fantasies, or a real estate hoax. Off the freeways, down the ramps, along the streets, through the markets, at the offices, in the homes, on the beaches, there was a vitality. Los Angeles was very alive and kicking. And it was not in black and white, but radiant Technicolor: brilliant blue skies, gorgeous golden sunshine, shocking pink houses, rich red-tiled roofs, pastel storefronts, incandescent colored billboards and flowers, shrubs and cars, and clothing of every hue.

To be sure, there was vulgarity, and trendy, vapid narcissism, as I had been warned. But there was also curiosity, concern, commitment and, particularly, a strong sense of the present and future. Whatever its age, Los Angeles seemed young, infectious. When William Butler Yeats visited Los Angeles in 1925, he remarked that "here, if anywhere else in America, I seem to hear the coming footsteps of the muse."

Whatever, I sensed what Carey Mc-

The incongruent suburban cityscape and architectural styles of
L.A. The adobe-styled home at
the base of the hill was built in
1986; most of the other houses
marching up the hill were built
in the 1960s and 1970s. These
houses seem oriented neither to
the site nor to their neighbors,
but rather to a remote view.

14

Below: The oceanfront, despite poor access, eroding cliffs, and cheek-to-jowl housing, is L.A.'s great gathering place, its sand-covered public piazza. This view is northwest from the Santa Monica palisades up the curving coast toward Malibu.

Bottom: A garden in the Holly-wood Hills fashioned out of a raw canyon. A semiarid desert backed up against the ocean, L.A. only needed to import plants and water in order to bloom.

16

Williams had written nearly a half century earlier in his classic *Southern California: An Island on the Land*, that "in all the world, there neither was nor would be another place like the City of the Angels. Here the American people were erupting, like lava from a volcano; here, indeed, was the place for me—a ringside seat at the circus."

What I have found, as I have embraced the city, is a marvelous mix of people, cultures, and scenes, out of which has grown a varied economy, and a stew of life-styles and landscapes, tempered with a tolerance that has made it distinctly American. Undoubtedly it is this spirit that lends the city the twinkle that can be seen on a clear night from Mulholland Drive or from a plane descending into the L.A. airport (LAX). It has also produced smog, sprawl, crime, crowded freeways, and other urban ills, as well as rampant, real estate speculation, economic disparities, and social and racial tensions.

All this did not happen overnight, as if some movie producer decided to add a "city" scene to a film and ordered a stage set to be erected in time for a morning shoot. Los Angeles has a unique history, growing from a desolate settlement of 44 persons in 1781 to 11,000 some 100 years later, then overcoming its natural limitations and, in a triumph of human will, evolving in fits and starts into one of the great cities of the world. Throughout its history, from the early days as a sporadic settlement, a cowtown, a boomtown, a resort, spurred on by imported water, the discovery of oil, motion-picture making, followed by the aircraft industry and continued migration, there has always been a rare sense of freedom, enhanced by an uninhibited rambunctiousness that has created some of the more distinctive architecture of the twentieth century. This book explores those forces that shaped and styled L.A.

As Los Angeles has grown to a region of 13 million people and enveloped the surrounding counties into a supersuburb bigger than many states, much of its characteristic architecture has unfortunately been lost. The long, sad list of landmarks, gone but not forgotten, includes grand mansions, detailed craftsman houses, personable bungalow courts, Moderne and Modern-styled homes, Art Deco stores, some marvelous roadside stands, magnificent civic structures, diverting amusement parks and piers, fabled film studios, and movie palaces. Lost also are the groves of oak trees that graced the landscape, the wild canyons, open beaches, what was once the world's most extensive interurban transit system and, here and there tucked away on hillsides, behind shopping centers, and near the beach, neighborhoods that lent Los Angeles a certain charm and identity. We mourn those landmarks.

But this book is not simply a lament about the social and architectural artifacts of a city that have disappeared. There is still much in the land- and cityscapes of Los Angeles to engage the eye and the spirit. Indeed, there has been a growing awareness and appreciation of the city's rich historic and creative legacy, and the need for its preservation and nurturing. It is these "found" landmarks and landscapes that lend Los Angeles a sense of time, place, and pride, and which this history also explores and celebrates.

1

THE SETTING

We entered a very spacious valley, well grown with cottonwoods and alders, among which ran a beautiful river from the north-northwest . . . It has all the requisites for a large settlement . . .

—Father Juan Crespi, diary entry, 1769

The first thing that catches your eye as you exit the airline terminal on a first visit to L.A. is a stand of Queen palm trees, parading like oddly shaped, bushy-topped telephone poles along the edge of a parking lot. For someone from New York City the palms look very exotic, like the opening scene of a tropical adventure film. But they are real, swaying in a refreshingly cool, early evening breeze that smells pleasantly of the salty ocean. And a little later as you drive on the freeway, looming up across the darkening horizon is a mountain range, which seems to be located in the middle of the city. For what was supposed to be a city, by definition a man-made environment, L.A. looks very natural.

Other surprises follow: the broad, inviting beaches, a sprawling coastal plain, verdant foothills, tortuous canyons, rugged mountains dropping precipitously into seemingly endless valleys, all within the city limits and all under a pervasive sun. But the palm trees are not indigenous (they have been imported from Mexico), neither are the stately, sweet-smelling eucalyptus (from Australia) that looked so at home nor most of the other trees, plants, and flowers decorating the L.A. landscape. But everything seems to thrive. Apparently all they need in the sandy soil under the Southern California sun are water and fertilizer (both also imported).

Certainly L.A.'s varied terrain is unique: a semiarid desert facing an ocean and encircled by four mountain ranges, the San Gabriels, San Bernardinos, San Jacintos, and Santa Susanas, and pierced by two more, the Santa Monicas and Santa Anas. The Spaniards simply called the ranges the Sierra Madre, for they did in so many ways mother the region. They provided the water and some plant life able to sustain a

Previous page opposite: A precept of L.A. real estate is that the closer to the water the more desirable and expensive the property. Overcoming legal and construction constraints, and not deterred by the threat of winter storm damage or high surf, houses embrace the oceanfront. The view from this house, designed by the firm of Buff/ Hensman, is of the Malibu shore.

rudimentary culture for the native Indians and early settlers. And by blocking off winter storms from the north and containing the sea breezes from the west, the mountains also generated a rare, insulated climate. The resulting semitropical weather, along with the fact that for years the mountains also impeded travel, prompted Southern California to be described by its early chroniclers as an "island on the land," a singular settlement that was to grow into a singular region.

While they lend the basins and valleys a feeling of space and are brilliant to look at, especially in the winter when they are snow topped, the mountains are not the dominant feature of L.A. Nor are the sandy beaches, stretching as they do for nearly a hundred miles from Malibu, where the Santa Monica Mountains meet the sea, to Laguna, and the San Joaquin Hills. There is no one dominant natural feature in L.A., such as the hills in San Francisco, Seattle, and Rome, the water in Hong Kong and Venice, or the mountain ranges astride Denver and Vancouver. Neither is there one dominant man-made feature, such as the skyline in New York and Chicago, the Eiffel Tower in Paris, and Big Ben in London. More than anything else what characterizes L.A. is its marvelous weather.

It is the weather that attracted the cattle ranchers to the region, followed by the farmers, retirees, tourists, moviemakers and movie hopefuls, hucksters, airplane manufacturers, automobile salesmen, migrants from the north and east, and immigrants from the south and west. And it is the weather that shaped L.A.'s distinct life-style and cityscape, endowing it with its seductive personality. As a real estate salesman is reported to have commented in the 1880s during the first of many land booms to sweep L.A., "we sold them the climate and threw the land in."

Fire in the hills of L.A., October 1978. The mountains in and about L.A. are quite susceptible to fire, particularly when fanned by the dry Santa Ana winds. This fire ravaged Agoura in October 1978. In that month fires in L.A. scorched 40,000 acres, destroyed 220 homes, and caused an estimated $100 million in damages.

The climate is quite varied, as indicated by the reports delivered on the local television news shows. Different forecasts are offered for the beaches, downtown, the east and west, inland valleys, the low and high deserts, and the mountains. And those are just simple, general forecasts. Meteorologists have noted that there are at least two dozen distinct microclimates in the L.A. region, with temperatures along the beach and coastal plain as much as 20 degrees cooler in the summer, and 10 degrees warmer in the winter, than in the interior valleys. Hillside climates also vary widely, depending on the play of sea breezes as they wend their way inland through the canyons, so that even neighbors may experience different weather patterns: one might be putting on a sweater in the evening and worrying about frost killing his tomato plants, while someone living a short distance downhill is swimming in a backyard pool. But while varying in the specific, the weather in general is quite consistent and, in a word, marvelous; a rare climate appropriately labeled Mediterranean, marked by mild winters, doused now and then by rain, and warm, dry summers.

That warm sun, when there is little or no breeze and quite a bit of pollution, particularly from vehicles, can create smog. Those mountain ranges tend to trap the pollution in the inland valleys so they can be cooked by the sun into a foul, unhealthy haze. Eyes smart, throats burn, voices rasp, and, for some, breathing becomes difficult, while the dirty, yellow-brown haze descends upon the city.

The warm sun's effect on extremely dry air out in the high deserts late in the summer or early autumn also creates a condition known as the Santa Ana winds, presumably named after the mountains they usually race through, to lash out across the city to the west. The winds, which have been known to reach velocities of up to 100 miles an hour, fan fires, create havoc, and generally get on everyone's nerves. In a short story appropriately titled "The Red Wind," Raymond Chandler described the arrival of the winds as a time when "every booze party ends in a fight," and "meek little wives feel the edge of the carving knife and study their husbands' necks," adding that "anything can happen. You can even get a full glass of beer at a cocktail lounge." Eve Babitz in *Slow Days, Fast Company* recalls that "when the Santa Anas were blowing so hard that searchlights were the only thing in the sky that were straight," she and her sister would run outside "and dance under the stars on our cool front lawn and laugh maniacally and sing 'hitch-hike, hitch-hike, give us a ride' imagining we could be taken up into the sky on broomsticks."

Santa Anas are most frightening and destructive when they combine with wildfires, another of L.A.'s environmental plagues. Fire always has been a part of the region's natural history, clearing underbrush and allowing select, native vegetation, such as chaparral, to regenerate. However, as housing has clambered into the hillsides and mountains, the fires have become more and more hazardous, having not only native brush to feed on, but also wood-shingle and shake roofs, redwood porches, and indiscriminate plantings of combustible shrubs and trees. The threat is further heightened by poor planning that allows houses to be scattered across the hillsides instead of clustered for better protection; by the stupidity of residents who barbecue during the fire season; by thoughtless drivers who, ignoring the signs, smoke while traveling through a fire zone; and, scariest, by arsonists. The combination has erupted into some disastrous conflagrations in recent years, which have killed dozens of people, injured hundreds of others, destroyed thou-

The constant search for building sites to serve a voracious real estate industry has produced developments that march up hillsides on spindly legs to perch precariously above L.A., as do these houses in Coldwater Canyon.

L.A.'s tiara of mountains is geologically young and fragile, and especially sensitive to fire and floods. Not a few homeowners have been awakened in the middle of a stormy night to find chunks of the surrounding landscape invading their house.

sands of homes, and spread fear across the city, along with the smoke and ashes.

The so-called fire season of late summer and early autumn is followed by the so-called rainy season, which stretches intermittently through the winter and during which it might even occasionally rain. The rains for the most part are welcome, adding to the limited, local water supply while giving L.A. a hint of seasons and some brilliant displays of wildflowers in the winter and spring. It is no coincidence that the annual Tournament of Roses was established before L.A. imported water or had hothouses and is held on New Year's Day.

But the rains also cause problems, especially if they come following a particularly bad fire season when hillsides have been denuded of plant life, or if the hillsides have not been graded properly to accommodate housing, or simply have had their natural form altered by such things as firebreaks, or, more seriously, off-road vehicles. The result has been some ruinous landslides in the hills and floods below on the plains.

And then, of course, there is always the threat of "the big one," which is what residents call the major earthquake that is predicted to hit the L.A. region at any time within the next month, year, decade, or millennium. Sitting on a spiderweb of seismic fault lines, L.A., along with the entire state of California, falls into the highest seismic-risk category in the world. Indeed, the city was severely shaken and disrupted by quakes in 1933 and 1971. Experts have predicted that the next major earthquake will be even more severe, and they have been urging the sluggish city to pick up the pace of enforcing more stringent building codes and inspections. Residents just hope they are not in an unreinforced masonry structure, or just outside one, when an earthquake hits.

The threat of "the big one" underlines the

Opposite: A protected and cultivated courtyard of the Hotel Bel Air. Nestled in Stone Canyon above Westwood, the luxury hotel and its lush grounds exude an image of a romantic, idealized Southern California.

Below: L.A.'s caressing weather and unique geography have combined to create some idyllic settings. This rustic pasture is tucked away in the mountains above Pasadena, its rock wall and wood gates reminiscent of the midwestern farms from which

the area's first settlers came. This pasture has been part of a working farm that was sold off for a housing development; depending on buyer interest and available financing, it may already have been bulldozed into history.

fragility of the entire L.A. landscape. "The land is restless here, restless and sliding," observes the narrator in the appropriately titled novel *The Slide Area,* by Gavin Lambert. And while the hillsides and mountains are particularly vulnerable to fires, floods, and landslides, the beach communities lay exposed to the threat of a tidal wave, touched off by a distant earthquake or offshore volcanic eruption. One has only to view the buildings crowding the ocean to contemplate the consequences. Also threatened by a combination of natural and unnatural acts are L.A.'s sandy shore, sensitive wetlands, and delicate deserts, each with their special ecology.

And then there has been man, who, basking in the climate, brought to the land water and technology, along with greed and fear, hopes and dreams.

Welcome to L.A.

2

EARLY YEARS

Los Angeles was not like some Middle-Western city that sinks its roots into some strategic area of earth and goes to work there. This was a lovely makeshift city. Even the trees and plants did not belong here. They came, like the people, from far places, some familiar, some exotic, all wanderers of one sort or another seeking peace or fortune or the last frontier, or a thousand dreams of escape.

—Frank Fenton: A *Place in the Sun* (1955)

Hiking in a chaparral-encrusted canyon deep in the Santa Monica Mountains, out of sight and sound of people and homes, or wandering through the remains of a mission, and even, occasionally, sitting on a tiled bench under the graceful Merton Bay fig tree in the Old Plaza downtown and looking west at the adobe facade of the Plaza church, one gets a sense of what L.A. and its environs were like when the Spaniards settled here a little over two hundred years ago: a stark, sun-drenched, sprawling landscape overwhelming a few sparse outposts. Measured by the history of cities, and considering the megalopolis into which L.A. has grown, that was not very long ago. Still, what makes L.A. more unusual than its relative youth and size is that it grew at all.

Pondering that question in the 1930s, when the population of the L.A. region stood at an estimated 2 million (compared to 12 million in 1985), Morris Markey wrote in *This Country of Yours* that "the Chamber of Commerce people told me about the concentration of fruit, the shipping, the Western-branch factories put up by concerns in the East. But none of these things seemed the cause of a city. They seemed rather the effect, rising from an inexplicable accumulation of people."

Markey concluded, "it struck me as an odd thing that here, alone of all the cities in America, there was no answer to the question, 'Why did a town spring up here, and why has it grown so big?' "

Actually, L.A. showed little promise as a city, let alone town, in its early years. When a Spanish expedition establishing missions along the California coast happened upon its site in 1769, it was a small Indian village called Yangna bordering a river, which a Father Juan

32

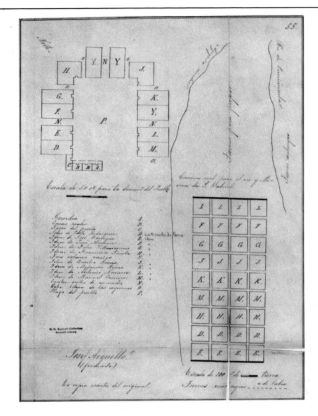

Crespi promptly christened "el Rio de Nuestra Senora la Reina de los Angeles de Porciuncula," the River of Our Lady the Queen of the Angels of Porciuncula (after St. Francis's chapel in Assisi). No mission was founded by the river, but the location, the promise of fertile soil, and the friendly natives were noted. And a dozen years later, on August 4, 1781, eleven families, following detailed directions of Governor Felipe de Neve, established an agricultural settlement there as part of imperialist Spain's colonization of California.

The "Pueblo de los Angeles" grew slowly, a cluster of raw one-story adobes, with their only distinctive characteristic being a tar roof. The tar came from the pits a few miles west, which still bubble today with escaping gases. Early accounts tell of a dusty, dirty pueblo, surrounded by flourishing wheat and corn fields, vineyards, and grazing lands. It was not until 1822, when the construction of a church on a new plaza was completed, that the pueblo actually began taking on the shape of a settled town. It was also in 1822 that California learned it was no longer a province of Spain but of an independent, more liberal Mexico. The secularization of the missions followed, with eight million acres being distributed through about 500 land grants, creating a countryside of rancheros and prompting L.A. to grow to about 1,650 residents, including 600 Indians. It was enough for the settlement to be officially declared a city by Mexico, but not enough to impress Richard Henry Dana. The Boston-bred author wandered ashore long enough in 1836 to write of his L.A. experience, in his classic *Two Years Before the Mast,* that he had been "in the remote parts of the earth, on an almost desert coast, in a country where there is neither law nor gospel."

Despite declaring its independence from Mexico in 1845, losing it briefly to Mexico in

A sketch of Los Angeles in 1854, then a dusty cowtown serving scattered ranchos. Prominent to the left are the church and plaza, but the grid prescribed by the Spanish sixty years earlier has already given way to random development. In the right foreground is a typical residence of the period, a one-story adobe structure with a flat roof no doubt covered with *brea* from the nearby tarpits.

1846, willingly succumbing to the Americans in 1847, being annexed by the United States in 1848, and then incorporated as a city in 1850 when California joined the Union, L.A. remained a very rough-and-tumble frontier town. With northern California flush with gold and paying top dollar for southern California cattle, L.A.'s rancheros prospered. But the prosperity also attracted bandits, gamblers, drifters, rustlers, and hustlers, causing the cowtown to be called for a while not "Los Angeles," the city of the angels, but "Los Diablos," the city of the devils, and the "City of Fallen Angels." Shootings and knifings were daily occurrences, with few persons being brought to justice. There were bullfights, gambling, prostitution, and, according to the chronicles of a minister, just about every type of heathen activity known.

For more than a decade into the 1860s, L.A. was an open frontier town (as tough as any that would be conjured up on a Hollywood back lot fifty years later). Then came the Civil War, along with a dwindling demand for cattle, followed by floods, a drought, a smallpox epidemic, and vigilantes, all dampening L.A.'s rough-hewn spirits. Slowly the rancheros with their vaqueros gave way to farms established by stolid migrants from the Midwest, but not before there was one last paroxysm of lawlessness: a race riot on October 26, 1871, in which nineteen Chinese were brutally murdered, following the death of a white policeman while trying to stop an ar-

The first buildings of distinction in Southern California were the missions, most of them crude adaptions of neo-Classical Mexican churches. Mission San Fernando *(opposite)* was erected in 1797, left to decay in the 1800s, and restored at the turn of the century, only to be severely damaged in the 1971 earthquake. An exact replica, including the mission's distinguishing arcade, was built in 1974. Mission San Gabriel *(below)* was established in 1771, and, after being moved and rebuilt of logs and then adobe, was destroyed in a flood in 1810. Rebuilt soon after with brick and stone, it has survived as a parish church.

gument between two Chinese gang members.

The riot sobered up L.A. The city's burgeoning and anxious middle class, led by its bankers, merchants, and land developers, realized that if the city did not generate an image of law and order, as well as industriousness, it should forever remain a "cowtown," diminishing both their investments and hopes. And generate a new image they did. Beginning in late 1872, they convinced the city of then about 5,500 inhabitants to underwrite a $602,000 subsidy to get the Southern Pacific Railroad to link L.A. to northern California and the rest of the country. (In the process they outflanked San Diego, whose natural harbor made it a more favorably located and logical terminus.) As expected, the prospects of the link, and the new settlers it would bring, in turn prompted a rash of new construction.

In 1867, L.A. had been described as "a town of crooked, ungraded, unpaved streets; low, lean, rickety, adobe houses, with asphaltum roofs, and here and there an indolent native, hugging the inside of a blanket." Ten years later, on September 6, 1876, when a golden spike was driven to complete the link and secure the last few feet of track, L.A. had the look and feel of a small, midwestern city. Its population had doubled to 11,000; the streets were paved; there were gas lamps; a city hall, along with a hospital, a public school, a college, a theater, and even an opera house had been built. There also were fine homes and hotels, among them the Pico House,

The Wolfskill orchard was established in 1841 when William Wolfskill planted two acres of orange trees on the edge of downtown L.A. Forty years later, when this print was made, the orchard covered more than 100 acres. In a few years it was to give way to a spreading city whose growth was spurred by a railroad happy to transport oranges east but happier to bring settlers west and sell them land.

Below: L.A. in the 1850s was a tough frontier town. This photograph was taken on Main Street in the early 1860s when civic leaders concerned with L.A.'s reputation and future were pressing for law and order. With the city prospering from the Civil War, two- and three-story brick buildings were beginning to rise, imitating structures with which settlers from the East and Midwest were familiar.

Bottom: The most monumental structure in L.A. in the 1860s was the central courthouse, in the so-called Temple Market block. Fashioned after Boston's Faneuil Hall, it was constructed by Jonathan Temple as a market house and theater. But soon after opening, the building's prominence prompted its use also as a courthouse. The clock tower was an early city landmark, which residents used to set their watches.

heast across Old Court House Hill

which still survives. The public buildings were of brick and Romanesque, forming solid reproductions of midwestern main streets, while the fashionable private houses were styled, not after the indigenous adobes, or the early missions, but instead mimicked the Italianate, Queen Anne, and Eastlake look then favored by the eastern-educated gentry. With prosperity came pretensions. As Kevin Starr observed in *Inventing the Dream*, the second volume of his history of California, by the end of the 1870s "the clock atop the Temple Block tower said in no uncertain terms that Los Angeles now ran on American time."

And in the 1880s it was Americans from across the country who in record numbers began flocking to L.A., attracted by the myths and promises of a more prosperous, healthier, interesting life in Southern California and aided in their quest by now relatively accessible rail links and inexpensive fares. The Sante Fe Railroad opened its line into L.A. in 1886 and almost immediately declared a rate war with the Southern Pacific. Each in turn then tried to undercut the other. Within months the passenger fare from Kansas City to L.A. plummeted from $125 to $12, and on March 6, 1887, dropped to as low as $1. According to a historical account of the period, "the result of this war was to precipitate such a flow of migration, such an avalanche rushing madly to Southern California as I believe has no parallel." In the year the rate war raged, an estimated 120,000 persons came west on the Southern Pacific alone. But, of course, there had to be at least a hint of something at the end of the rainbow to prompt people to get on those trains to L.A. and take a look. And there was.

Extolling Southern California for years as a place to live better and longer had been a variety of popular books and pamphlets.

About 1880 — City Hall and Jail — Northwest corner Spring and Franklin St.

The city hall and jail in 1880 *(opposite top)* was a rough-hewn structure that lent its walls to advertisements and shared its space. But other construction boomed. Office buildings and stores designed in commercial Italianate, Romanesque, and Gothic styles rose to give downtown a look of substance. The photograph *(opposite bottom)* of Broadway and Second Street was taken in 1889. The flag had been hung to celebrate the opening of the cable car route up Second Street to the new housing subdivisions to the west.

Published in 1859, *Climatology of the United States*, by Lorin Blodget, compared the climate of Southern California with that of Italy and prescribed it for those suffering consumption, asthma, and rheumatism. Charles Nordoff went further, as indicated in the title of his 1872 best-seller, *California for Health, Pleasure and Residence* (a book not coincidentally written while on a junket subsidized by the Southern Pacific in anticipation of its line into L.A.). Charles Dudley Warner declared, "Children cut teeth here without trouble and disorders of the liver and kidneys are rare." A Dr. Peter Remondino added, "From my personal observations I can say that at least an extra ten years' lease on life is gained by a removal to this coast from the Eastern states: not ten years to be added with its extra weight of age and infirmity, but ten years more with additional benefits of feeling ten years younger during the time." These were enticing comments for an eastern and midwestern America then in the throes of a gritty industrial revolution creating overcrowded, dirty, gray cities, rank with a host of illnesses.

Health seekers who could afford to flocked to Southern California, prompting the construction of hotels, resorts, and sanitariums, and earning for L.A. for a while the title of "Capital of the Sanitarium Belt." Observing the migration to L.A. and environs was David Starr Jordan, the founding president of Stanford University. He recalled that "the Pullman cars in the winter used to be full of sick people, banished from the East by physicians who did not know what else to do with their incurable patients." In his history *The Health Seekers of Southern California, 1870 – 1900*, John Baur declared that "for the first time in American history, a frontier was developed by the sickly and invalid."

Baur should have preceded "sickly and invalid" with "wealthy," for whatever their varying illnesses, most also were people of means, who could afford to relocate and recuperate. These were very comfortable immigrants, not coming to Southern California to put up a mud hut and scratch out an existence for a few years, running up the bill at the local general store. They had money to build attractive homes, hire help, host banquets, direct charities, and form social, economic, and political networks. Though they might have been sickly, "many of these early settlers were people of enterprise, talent, intellect and culture," commented social historian Carey McWilliams, adding that they also had the wealth to direct these virtues into a civic vision. But the infirm were certainly not the only migrants the railroads, land speculators, and civic boosters hoped to attract. If readers had not gotten the message in the title to Nordoff's book, Jerome Madden made it a little blunter in his 1890 effort, *California: Its Attractions for the Invalid, Tourist, Capitalist, and Homeseeker.*

While Pasadena and Sierra Madre to the north, Riverside to the east, and Santa Monica to the west of L.A. were getting reputations as resorts suitable for both the comfortable and the consumptive, L.A. itself was still very much a farm town, albeit a growing and prosperous one. "No happier paradise for the farmer can be found than Los Angeles County," wrote Ludwig Salvador in 1872, in the first of many glowing reports on the potential of Southern California's agriculture. "Almost everything grown on earth can be raised in Los Angeles County. The pomegranate flourishes side by side with the potato, the banana with the tomato, the orange, lime and apricot with the peach, pear and apple. The guava and the plum, the olive and the squash, are found in Los Angeles County, in the most loving com-

Below: By 1890, L.A. had a new city hall and police station. The civic complex seen in the center of the photograph is marked by a Romanesque tower. *Bottom:* The tower, from which the photo-graph was taken in 1890, offered sweeping views to the west and the expanding residential community on Bunker Hill and the varied styles of the houses there.

Bottom: By 1905, when this photograph was taken looking up Spring Street from Third Street, L.A. had established itself as a major city with a bustling downtown. The sidewalks were jammed with shoppers and the streets with every type of transportation, dominated by horse-drawn carriages and wagons and the electric streetcars, the so-called red and yellow cars of the interurban system. In the lower left a lone horseless carriage, a modest augur of things to come, can be seen.

panionship side by side," rhapsodized Maj. Ben Truman in his *Tourist Illustrated Guide to California*, published in 1883. The hype became so heavy that one wag commented that in Southern California farming consisted of "irrigating, cultivating and exaggerating." Exaggerated or not, it was a vision that restless farmers in the Midwest and East, waiting out the dark, long winters there, could not resist.

According to turn-of-the-century essayist Hildegarde Hawthorne, it was the "Middle Westerner" who was especially fascinated: "If he had money and youth, he came to buy and to grow. If he had money and was old, he came to rest and go right on living. If he was an invalid, he came to be cured—and usually was. He brought his wife and family along if he had them. Often, too, he or she brought some queer religious leanings along, or a whole sect came in a lump."

Adding the critical element of romance to color the image of Southern California was Helen Hunt Jackson's novel, *Ramona*. The melodramatic tale of star-crossed Indian lovers in the waning days of the proud Spanish rancheros, beset by avaricious Americans, became a best-seller in 1884. As historian Kevin Starr suggested in *Inventing the Dream*, the novel gave Southern California "a myth by which to know itself." Here for dreamers reading in the rude, dank eastern cities or in bland, boring midwestern towns was a view of a sunny arcadia, an enchanted land of warm winters and rich traditions. And if this wasn't enough, there also was the image of Southern California as a new Mediterranean paradise being suggested in tourist guides and the emigrant's proverbial letters home.

Waiting in 1887 to meet the health seekers, farmers, tourists, and dreamers flocking to L.A. were an estimated two thousand real estate agents peddling five hundred thou-

As the interurban system expanded, so did the development and enjoyment of the region. The system was used during the week by commuting workers and on weekends for outings by social groups and families. *Opposite top:* Cyclists at a siding in Pasadena who have just gotten off the streetcar with their bicycles. Pasadena was a popular tourist area, attracting day groups from L.A. and winter vacationers from the East and Midwest. To serve the tourists, various resorts were built, many of which were modeled after fashionable eastern establishments. One of the more impressive was the Raymond Hotel *(opposite bottom),* which opened in 1886 but burned to the ground in 1895.

sand building lots in hundreds of "paper" towns, projecting a total population of 2 million. Within a year the boom fizzled; many of the migrants drifted back home or elsewhere. Still, L.A.'s population had exploded to nearly fifty thousand. Growth had become the city's prime industry.

The challenge now was not how to tame or shape the city, but how to continue the growth. A concerted publicity campaign, directed by a determined and resourceful chamber of commerce, promoted L.A. in the 1890s as no other city, product, or candidate, war or referendum had ever been promoted before. There were traveling exhibits sent on special trains to towns and cities across the country, lavish displays at every possible exposition and fair, and millions of pieces of promotional literature distributed everywhere, including the frozen Klondike, to attract south the newly minted millionaires who had just struck gold there. A quality magazine was underwritten, *Land of Sunshine,* edited by the flamboyant Charles Fletcher Lummis, to call attention to Southern California's burgeoning cultural scene, which he and a few other eastern-educated transplants were nurturing.

The most exuberant pitch came at the 1893 Colombian Exposition in Chicago, in which L.A.'s master publicist, Frank Wiggins, wangled the best exhibit space for Southern California and turned it into a garden of earthly delights. "If you dangle a golden orange before the eyes of a Northern man you can lead him anywhere," Wiggins remarked. In the course of the fair he dangled an estimated 375,000 oranges, giving so many cartloads away on opening day that guards had to be brought in to maintain order. As a result, the California pavilion was one of the most successful at the popular fair, and Southern California's exhibit, including a real citrus orchard, as well as a prune-encrusted knight on horseback, and a giant pyramid of raisins, was the most highly attended. "California enshrined the purple and gold of her sun-kissed fruit with the nation's colors, and scattered in the lap of the world the treasures of her vineyards," declared the *Chicago Times.* "There is an air of prosperity and abundance about it all that is seen in no other state building."

It was also in the 1890s that the nation's newspapers began reporting on an odd New Year's Day celebration in Pasadena, where, while most of the rest of the country shivered, Southern Californians held a floral parade, dubbed the Tournament of Roses, usually in balmy weather. The promotions attracted a steady stream of migrants. By the turn of the century L.A.'s population had grown to about 103,000. As its boosters beamed and prospered, L.A. at last began taking on the shape and character of a city.

Still a bit dusty from its cowtown days, and dowdy from its recent influx of midwesterners, L.A. was awkwardly emerging from the shadow of the "other" California city, San Francisco. The sun and publicity served L.A. well, warming its spirit for the decades ahead.

Overleaf: The interior court of the Bradbury Building. This building was designed by George Wyman and built in 1893. With its glass-covered court, ornate cast-iron and wood-encrusted balconies, and open stairs and caged elevators, the commercial structure was unique for its time and setting. It still is.

3

EARLY STYLES

I just got off the Sunset Train,
I'm from the Angel Town,
The Golden West Los Angeles,
Where the sun shines all year 'round.
I left a girlie back there,
She's the sweetest girl I Know,
She said "good-bye," I'll wait for you,
In the land of the bungalow.

Chorus:
In the Land of the Bungalow,
Away from the ice and snow,
Away from the cold,
To the Land of the Gold,
Away where the poppies grow,
Away to the setting sun,
To the home of the orange blossom,
To the land of fruit and honey,
Where it does not take much money,
To own a bungalow.

I just can't keep my thoughts away,
from California's shores,
The land of flowers and winter showers,
How I miss you more and more.
As soon as I can get away,
I know that I will go back to the girl I love best,
In the land of the Bungalow.

—George Devereaux, "In the Land of the Bungalow" (Circa 1900)

Name an architectural style and L.A. has it. On select, single blocks in L.A., one can see an encyclopedic range of structures: from simple adobes, cute Queen Annes, modest bungalows, and minimal ranch houses to florid Victorians, sprawling Spanish Colonials, contentious French chateaux, curious Georgians, massive Modernes, dainty Art Decos, sleek Moderns, and all sorts of eclectic and neo-eclectic experiments, outrages, and vernacular variations. No row upon row of anonymous brownstone and brickfronts here. A few of the more formal, columned structures looked as if they had been designed or inspired by the Italian master Andrea Palladio, others by Irving Gill, Frank Lloyd Wright, a playful Charles Moore, or Walt Disney, and still more by childhood memories or adult aberrations.

The variety of styles is very much in the eclectic tradition of L.A., which ever since its founding seems to have been searching for a distinguishing architecture. "Finding ourselves in a new environment, we owe it to ourselves, not less than to the country of our adoption, to continue its traditions by a careful study of the new conditions which we find and the history back of them," declared Myron Hunt in 1907 as he settled in to become one of Southern California's more prolific and accomplished architects. Twenty years later, Hunt, in an article entitled "Personal Sources of Pacific Coast Architectural Development," was deploring how real estate speculators jumped "from one fad to another," followed by local architects mimicking various European styles.

The situation has not changed very much. The history of architecture in L.A. has been a history of adapting styles to the local environment and market: styles from Europe, Asia, the East Coast, Mexico, or even the San Francisco Bay area. Over the years, numerous styles have come and gone, each leaving its mark. A few have also endured.

Limited by local materials and a lack of architectural skills, the first structures in L.A., after the domed thatched huts of the Indians, were simple adobes. Consisting of unfired bricks of straw and mud, which tended to melt into a mass of mud if not protected from heavy rains, the early adobes in L.A. were marked by their relatively flat roofs of matted brush, which were coated with brea from the tar pits. The romantic vision of early L.A. as a red-tile-topped settlement in the Spanish tradition is a bit blurry, for the firing of tiles was a long and expensive process and used only

With L.A. becoming more American and prosperous, the early, raw adobe residential style gave way in the 1850s to the Monterey style, which featured, as in the design of the Lugo Ranch House in Bell Gardens, walls of adobe and cantilevered second-floor wooden balconies.

The Monterey style, in turn, was replaced in popularity by the more studied and detailed Italianate style. One of the more prominent Italianate structures was the John Forthmann House, at Eighteenth and Figueroa streets, seen in an 1880s photograph.

Also popular at the time was the Greek Revival style.

L.A., with no particular architectural style, prompted settlers of means in the late nineteenth century to simply exercize their fantasies based on various picturesque designs then in vogue in the East. The designs came under the general heading of Victorian, with variations being labeled more precisely Queen Anne, Eastlake, or, more colorfully, romantic Romanesque, Châteauesque, or simply gingerbread. These styles were distinguished by irregular designs, porches and balconies, a clutter of detailed shingles, columns and arches, and, in particular, roofs with confusions of towers, turrets, gables, and dormers. Examples range from the relatively staid Miller/Herriott House in North University Park *(below)* to the more substantial home of May Rindge, on South Harvard Boulevard *(bottom)*.

sparingly for select missions. Wood, also, was scarce, having to be shipped in and subject to heavy import duties by the Mexicans. The most distinguished structure in L.A. during its early years was the church Nuestra Senora de Los Angeles (Our Lady of the Angels), generally known, because of its location, as the Plaza church. It was first completed in 1822, and has been altered and reoriented several times, including in 1861 when heavy rains washed away its adobe facade. There was not very much more to L.A. as it evolved from a raw Spanish settlement, to a raw Mexican pueblo, to a raw American frontier town.

"The site of Los Angeles is lovely, but the city is very ugly," wrote a settler fresh from the East in 1852. "Most of the houses are built of mud, some are plastered on the outside and have a porch around them looking neat and pretty as any house, but these are few." The few became many over the next two decades as wood became more plentiful, and the adobe gave way to the Monterey style, a blend of adobe and New England construction, with some Greek-Revival and Federal detailing. Often rising to two stories, and adorned by wooden balconies and verandas, the Monterey-style house matured to become a very characteristic Californian structure, a bit rough-edged and open, like the frontier itself. But it made the new American settlers uncomfortable, and when they had the means, they turned to the more familiar and acceptable, ornate styles then favored in the East, principally Italianate, replete with pedimented and hooded windows, bay where possible, cornices, and other ornaments. Cheap lumber from the north and cheap labor from the south aided the fad, which consumed quite a bit of both.

The Italianate style of the late 1860s and 1870s dominated commercial as well as resi-

Among the more extravagant examples was the Bradbury residence crowning Bunker Hill. It was built in 1890, three years before the construction of the landmark commercial building downtown that bears the owner's name.

The most ambitious civic building of the late nineteenth century was the County Courthouse, reflecting in its robust Richardson Romanesque style the pride and vanity of an emerging city. Designed in 1888 by Theodore Eisen of the firm Curlett and Cuthbertson, the fortresslike structure topped by a red sandstone clock tower opened in 1891, replacing the court housed in the Temple Market block. About twenty years later, in 1910, the courthouse was deemed too small and another building was constructed to handle the overflow. Damaged by the 1933 earthquake, it was demolished in 1936.

dential growth, and L.A., which only a few years before had been a cowtown, began to look like a settled farming center in the midwestern corn belt. One of the grander constructions was Pico House, a hotel ironically financed by Pio Pico, the last Mexican governor, to serve as a showpiece and social center to impress the Anglos, then beginning to stream into Southern California. L.A. was changing fast, but not without cost. To make way for his hotel, Pico had to buy and demolish his brother-in-law's house, which since the 1820s had been one of L.A.'s finer structures. The *Los Angeles News* of September 7, 1869, noted: "The old tile-covered house on the corner of Main and the Plaza is being torn down and removed, and a first-class hotel is to be erected on the lot by the owner thereof, Pio Pico. Thus, one by one, the old landmarks are disappearing, and Los Angeles will soon have few things to remind the visitor that she is one of the oldest cities on the Pacific Coast."

With the waves of the new migrants from the East during the boom of the 1880s and 1890s came the waves of new eastern architectural styles, albeit a few years late. The classical and controlled Italianate was followed by the stolid neo-Romanesque style of the larger commercial and public buildings. Among the more notable of these structures were the City Hall and the County Courthouse, the latter marked by a massive, red sandstone clock tower. Most of the commercial efforts were undistinguished, with the exquisite exception of the Bradbury Building designed by George Wyman and constructed in 1893. With its soaring, skylighted, bright interior court, rich wrought-iron railings and grills, and yellow-glazed brick walls, the building remains one of the most delightful architectural experiences downtown.

In residential architecture, Italianate gave way to a variety of romantic and picturesque Victorian styles, principally Queen Anne and Eastlake, and curious mixes of both. As in most new communities with few traditions and less social structure, houses became the symbol of a person's worth—you are what you buy or build. As a result, the Victorian styles with their wide variety of shapes and decorations became a popular format for owners to express their pretensions: the more "gingerbread," the more wealth. With little regard for siting and climate, some of the ornate structures were overwhelming, perched like elephants on stools. They also were expensive to build and maintain, and eventually fell out of favor.

Among recent arrivals there was a subtle and growing self-awareness, along with an emerging pride, that L.A. was not Cleveland, Kansas City, or Des Moines, though its downtown might look it. These people had come to Southern California to seek a new, healthier, more relaxed existence in a comfortable climate, and somehow their homes should support and reflect that life-style. Out of that search for a more expressive and, not coincidentally, less expensive, residential architecture came the California bungalow.

A variation on a basic native dwelling in India known as "Bangala," and its adaptation by the British, the simply styled, box-like, wood bungalow, with a porch or porches, was cozy in the winter and cool in the summer, and fit very comfortably into the L.A. landscape. It was also reasonably priced, with a few of the more basic designs lifted out of pattern books and costing less than a $1,000 to construct. "The bungalow was practical, and it also symbolized for many the best in the good life," declared Robert Winter in his study, *The California Bungalow*. "As easterners came west, they found bungalows waiting for them,

The search for an appropriate architectural style for the region continued through the turn of the century, with confusing results. The Garfield School (opposite top) in Pasadena, built in the early 1900s, included bits, pieces, and themes of a half dozen styles, from its Romanesque arches to its Queen Anne roof. A similar mix was reflected in a row of flats built a few years later on Figueroa Street (opposite bottom), where Greek, Georgian, Federal, and Mission Revival styles presented an eclectic façade.

either for rent for a few months, or more often to call home. In fact, the great sprawl of the city of Los Angeles is as much a testimony to the popularity of the simple little house set in its garden as it is to the fad of the automobile . . . The bungalow contributed to the privacy considered sacred by the middle class. The feeling of independence it gave, even on a tiny plot of land, is part of the freedom which even today one senses in Southern California."

As the popularity of the bungalow was growing so was that of the Arts and Crafts movement. Begun in England as a reaction to a harsh industrialization, the movement called for an idealized, simple life, respectful and reflective of local environment, history, and culture, a dedication to the revival of handicraft, and an all encompassing architecture of "sweetness and light." It was a philosophy that was very well suited to the growing, enlightened, middle and upper classes that were settling in a relatively rustic Southern California at the turn of the century. The bungalow was just a bit too basic, too déclassé. The settlers wanted a home more symbolic of their new, pastoral existence.

The strongest devotees of the Arts and Crafts movement tended to live northeast of downtown L.A., toward Pasadena, along the Arroyo Seco, prompting the label, the "Arroyo culture." The ubiquitous writer, editor, folklorist, and promoter Charles Fletcher Lummis was its most prominent booster. It was a heady time for a young, L.A. pseudo-intelligentsia searching through the traditions of the missions and Mediterranean cultures for roots, if not just for some decorations for its romantic myths.

In Pasadena, which had become a haven for the wealthy, the Arts and Crafts movement took on an even more genteel veneer. It combined the social graces and prejudices of the East with a sincere appreciation of the local environment and presented them with a studied informality. It was here, during the halcyon decade at the beginning of the new century, that the bungalow style blossomed into the Craftsman style.

The style was dedicated to the proposition that good design involved good craftmanship, and that it should envelop man as a total experience and not simply be applied as ornamentation. "I seek till I find what is truly useful, then I try to make it beautiful," explained Charles Sumner Greene, who with his brother, Henry Mather Greene, became the movement's premier artists. Every detail in the planning of their Craftsman-styled houses appears to have been carefully considered, from such major decisions as siting, scale, and massing, to the more minor but no less critical decisions such as whether the brass screws fastening the interior, wood trim should be covered with square pegs of ebony, mahogany, or oak. With interiors of delicately joined, hand-sculptured, and polished wood, exquisite Tiffany lamps, and individually crafted furnishings, the houses were truly works of art.

One of the more sublime Greene and Greene designs was for David Gamble (of Proctor and Gamble wealth), who had retired to Pasadena and, in the spirit of the time and place, wanted a comfortable home that would take advantage of the area's benign weather. He sought a design along the lines of an unostentatious, woodsy house (but wanted it executed with elegance) and wanted plenty of room for servants, guests, and large parties, that could move with ease between the house and the landscaped gardens. In short, what he wanted was something to give form to an idealized vision of bucolic life in Southern California. The result was the Gamble House, which has been described by its curator and chroni-

Gaining increasing popularity in the early 1900s was the Mission style, with its flexible stucco construction, distinctive arches, terra-cotta ornamentation, and romantic allusions to the region's Spanish and Mexican history.

The style was applied with flair to a range of buildings, including the home of architect John Parkinson *(opposite left)*, the Riverside Library *(opposite right)* and the sprawling Mission Inn *(below)*.

cler, Randell Makinson, as the "ultimate bungalow."

But just how "honest" the bungalow and its Craftsman variations were was another matter. As an expression of a certain life-style, the bungalow was quite appropriate to L.A. As an expression of the region's architectural and cultural history, however cloudy, it was not. "It is broadly true that the average house here is artistically and in convenience an improvement upon the (Eastern) house," declared social arbitrator Charles Fletcher Lummis in an 1895 edition of his then influential journal, *Land of Sunshine*. But, he added, "not one new house in a thousand here has learned anything locally. It is still the house of three-foot snows and zero weather, of summer rains, of forest, humid countries—grafted upon a semi-tropic soil whose sky is that of the Arid Lands. Its only adaptation to the new conditions is a pitiful little more of porch and a cheaper construction—since it no longer has to be burglar-proofed against the air of heaven, nor arteried with furnace-pipes." The construction material of the bungalow was principally wood, which in semiarid Southern California was difficult to find and was at risk to termites and dry rot.

As part of a campaign to get L.A. to acknowledge its Spanish heritage, a campaign that would consume most of his active life, Lummis advocated an adobe style. This not only included the use of adobe bricks, but classic, Spanish, design elements like thick walls, enclosed courtyards, and lush landscaping. And, in keeping with the campaign, Lummis and others associated with the Arroyo Culture were also urging the preservation and restoration of the most prominent architectural symbols of romantic Southern California, the missions. Their efforts led to the formation in 1895 of the California Landmarks Club,

An ornate Craftsman, hinting of
an Oriental influence.

A Craftsman bungalow, with low-
pitched roof, exposed struts and
beams, stone fireplace and foundation, and porches.

Bungalow courts provided
affordable, urban housing.

The emergence of the Bungalow style at the turn of the century served the need for inexpensive housing. The early bungalows were not much more than simple wood-frame houses, the many designs of which were taken from pattern books and easily adapted to the benign climate and sprawling landscape of the L.A. region. The straightforward designs and extensive use of wood (then flooding Southern California from the Northwest) also conjured up an image of a rural, rustic life-style in the spirit of the frontier. The image was embraced by the new settlers, who longed to sit on the open porches of the bungalows and watch the orange trees grow. As the orange trees grew, so did the houses, blossoming into the California Bungalow style.

one of the first preservationist groups in the nation.

Not only were many of the missions saved, but interest in the style also was spurred. It had been used quite successfully as a symbol of a tradition-rich, sunny arcadia by Arthur Page Brown (with an assist by a young Bernard Maybeck) in the California State Building at the 1893 exposition held in Chicago. With the blessing of Lummis and other commentators of the day, the plain stucco walls, arches, red-tiled roofs, and, wherever possible and sometimes impossible, a bell tower or a dome were soon being adapted to resort hotels, schools, train stations, and a variety of other public buildings. For nearly twenty years, a long time for any architectural style, what had come to be called Mission Revival dominated the architectural scene in L.A.

Although designers like Irving Gill tried almost desperately to update Mission Revival into a purer, more functional mode, purer it did not get. Instead it led quite directly to the more elaborate Spanish Colonial Revival style. Characterized by rich terra-cotta and cast-concrete ornamentation (known as Churrigueresque, after its original applicator, José de Churriguera), the style was introduced at the Panama-California Exposition staged in San Diego in 1915. Applying the style with a flair to the California State Building was Bertram Grosvenor Goodhue, who had wrested the commission away from Gill with the promise of delivering a design embodying "the romance of the old Spanish civilization" with the adventure and spirit of the new California. That indeed Goodhue did, designing the building in the form of a great cathedral, topped by a tile dome, topped in turn by a wrought-iron weather vane in the shape of a Spanish man-of-war. The style was launched.

Seeded in Baroque Spain and cultivated in Renaissance Mexico, the new style flowered in eclectic Southern California. Entire towns embraced it for official buildings, while large and small developers and their obliging architects applied it with increasing imagination, for better and worse, to every conceivable project, from commercial strips to residential tracts. Today the style still dominates stretches of streets, so that, when driving past in the heat of a midday sun, whole blocks seem a blur of white stucco, red-tile roofs, and shimmering ornamentation. By 1920 the design motif was being referred to not as Spanish Revival, Spanish Baroque, or Moorish, but simply the California style.

Whatever it was called, the style gave form to a persistent Southern California myth: that given its climate the region was indeed America's Mediterranean and should adapt the best the ancient cultures there could offer. The style reflected quite well the growth L.A. experienced in the early 1900s. It was exuberant, flexible, and decorative, at times applied with a heavy hand and at others playfully.

While the Mission and Spanish motifs dominated residential and civic design in the early 1900s, the downtown business community was, as usual, more traditional. It pursued the Beaux Arts image of the forthright, decorative, classical-styled halls of commerce then favored in New York by the fashionable architectural firm of McKim, Mead and White, which was also being copied in aspiring downtowns and civic centers across the country. Happily, the style was copied well by John Parkinson and other architects in L.A., where a series of substantial, well-decorated, and detailed office and bank buildings rose to form an area centered on Spring Street known as the "Wall Street of the West." With rich, terra-cotta encrusted exteriors, fluted Corinthian

Charles and Henry Greene combined the concern of the Craftsman aesthetic for materials and the California Bungalow style for simplicity with touches of the Orient and genius in a series of houses, most of them built in Pasadena for wealthy clients. One of the brothers' more sublime creations was the Gamble House *(below)*, completed in 1908. Each detail seems to have been carefully considered, right down to the hand-sculpted and polished joinery *(opposite)*.

columns, ornate cornices, domed corner towers, and marble and stained glass lobbies, the buildings declared their wealth and stability.

The commercial structures were designed in the so-called City Beautiful mold, a high-minded vision of a neo-Classical, well-ordered city that had arisen out of the 1893 exposition in Chicago to capture the imagination of civic leaders. One result of this new consciousness was an ordinance approved in 1905 that limited building heights to 150 feet. The ordinance, which remained in force for fifty-two years, was not a result of fears of earthquakes (the disastrous San Francisco quake would come a year later in 1906), but of concern for the city's aesthetics and quality of

Below: By 1905, when this photograph of Lincoln Heights northeast of downtown was taken, the suburban landscape of L.A. was already taking on a rich, eclectic, sprawling character. In the Heights can be seen bungalows and a variety of Italianate- and Queen Anne-styled houses.

Below: While the Mission and the more ornate romantic Mediterranean styles were being adapted for civic buildings, the city's commercial interests were embracing the decorative, classical Beaux Arts movement. One of the grander examples of the day was the Pacific Mutual Building, designed in 1906 by John Parkinson and Edwin Bergstrom.

life. L.A. was to be "a place of inspiration for nobler living," declared Dana Bartlett, a local civic leader at the time. Bartlett published a book in 1907 entitled *The Better City*, in which he envisioned L.A. as an egalitarian model of the City Beautiful.

Inspired by Barlett and others, idealized proposals flourished over the next decade. They called for an elaborate civic center, public squares, public baths, parks, playgrounds, promenades, parkways, and other municipal improvements. Unfortunately, they could not keep up with the reality of the boom years that followed, and hopes for the City Beautiful were to be overwhelmed by the City Bountiful.

4

BOOM TOWN

What the gold rush had been to Northern California, the real-estate-oil-and-motion picture boom was to Southern California. The great boom of the 'eighties had been spectacular, but it had been limited to land speculation. The boom of the 'twenties, on the other hand, was a truly bonanza affair. Millions of dollars in new income poured into Los Angeles, undermining the social structure of the community, warping and twisting its institutions, and ending in a debacle (the stock market crash) . . . . For Southern California the decade was one long drunken orgy, one protracted debauch.

—Carey McWilliams, *Southern California: An Island on the Land* (1946)

In the early 1920s when Max and Yetta Shulman went on a Sunday outing with their five children, it was usually to Venice, then a beckoning, beach-town playland and, as it is now, a place to promenade. The trip, from Boyle Heights in the rolling hills east of downtown, where the Shulmans lived, to seaside Venice, took about an hour on the interurban electric railway. They traveled first to downtown on a yellow car for 5 cents, then changed to a red car for the 10-cent ride to the Windward Avenue terminal and Abbott Kinney's popularized version of Italian Venice. But before they could walk beneath the arcades and glimpse the thousand and one attractions, buy an ice-cream square, or a twist of taffy off a "hokey poke" cart, consider a gondola ride, or, more likely, just stroll on the beach, Max first had to contend with the real estate salesmen.

"They were always a dozen or more there to greet us when we got off the trolley," recalls Max's son, Julius Shulman, then a wide-eyed preteen. "They were dressed in suits and hats, and offered us a free lunch if we would just take a drive with them in their Model T cars and look at some of the building lots that were for sale along the canals. We sometimes rode in their cars, ate their sandwiches, looked at the lots, but never bought. We already had a house." No matter, the salesmen smiled and moved on. There were also hundreds of thousands of other prospects. There were also tens of thousands of real estate agents.

"In 1849 sailors abandoned their ships in San Francisco Bay to rush to the California gold fields. In 1922 and 1923 white-collar clerks in Southern California everywhere deserted good office jobs to become real estate salesmen," observed W. W. Robinson, an intrepid commentator of the period. He noted that, almost every weekend, every tract devel-

The turn-of-the-century vision of Southern California as the American Mediterranean was given form by Abbott Kinney in his fanciful development of a strip of L.A. oceanfront he christened Venice. The arcaded buildings seen in a 1906 photograph *(opposite)* were designed by Norman Marsh and C. H. Russell in an Italian Renaissance style and led from the last stop on the Red Car line to the beach. Venice covered hundreds of acres and included a variety of entertainment and cultural facilities *(below)* focused on man-made lagoons. There also were miles of canals featuring gondolas and gondoliers *(bottom)* imported from Italy. Flanking the canals were homesites Kinney hoped to sell, for while a popular attraction, Venice also was a residential subdivision competing with numerous others rising to meet the demands of a burgeoning population.

65

Previous page opposite: Oil wells crowding out houses and palm trees northwest of downtown at the turn of the twentieth century.

oper would sponsor some real estate promotion or other, be it free dishes in Culver City, a barbecue in Hollywood, a concert in Palos Verde Estates, or an air show in Venice.

With a free lunch as his inducement, Robinson, one morning, took a ride out Wilshire Boulevard with a real estate salesman, who tried to sell him some lots on the West Side. "Follow my advice and buy one, or ten, of these lots, regardless of the sacrifice it might mean," declared the salesman, according to an account by Robinson. "Ten thousand banks may close, stocks may smash, bonds may shrink to little or nothing, but this tract and Los Angeles real estate stands like the Rock of Gibraltar for safety, certainty and profit. Don't be satisfied with six percent on your money. Don't be satisfied with twelve percent. Buy property like this and keep it, and as sure as the world moves it will pay you one hundred percent to one thousand percent." Though Robinson didn't indicate whether he bought anything, the salesman's predictions were quite prescient, no doubt, much to his surprise.

The Shulmans had come to L.A. from Connecticut in 1920, first purchasing a house northwest of downtown and then two years later in Boyle Heights. The Shulmans were but drops in an enormous wave of immigrants flooding L.A. From 1900 to 1920, L.A.'s population grew from about 103,000 to 575,000, and another 325,000 in the surrounding county. But the real boom was just starting. In a few short years, as more than 100,000 people streamed annually into the region, the boom became the largest migration in the history of America. It was described as everything from a gentle transplanting of a genteel bourgeoisie to "a swarm of invading locusts." By 1930 the population of the L.A. region was estimated at 2.2 million. And it was no longer principally

Venice's initial success attracting crowds and selling homesites spurred similar developments along the L.A. oceanfront. This exotic bathhouse, fashioned after those in Brighton, England, and combined with cafés and a casino, was located in Ocean Park just north of Venice.

the weather and farming that was spurring the migration, as they had at the turn of the century. Now oil strikes, the fledgling movie industry, tourism, and the momentum of the growth itself were drawing easterners to this new Manifest Destiny.

Pacing the growth was the sprawling Pacific Electric transit system. "It would never do for an electric line to wait until the demand for it came," declared the line's owner, Henry Edward Huntington. "It must anticipate the growth of communities and be there when the home builders arrive—or they very likely are not to arrive at all, but go to some other section already provided with arteries of traffic." Huntington also owned a real estate company with extensive land holdings served by the electric line, and it was these land sales that in effect subsidized the Pacific Electric as it grew to a 1,164-mile network to become, in its time, the largest interurban system in the nation. Some developers gave away kitchen appliances or golf-club memberships to purchasers of their houses; Huntington gave them accessible, relatively inexpensive mass transit. Though not an original gimmick, it was an effective one.

Wherever streetcars went in L.A., communities grew. Just as development today in the suburbs and beyond tends to follow new highways, development then followed trolley tracks. The city's first system was a horse-drawn affair that ran south during the 1870s to what is now University Park. L.A.'s first suburb was created, an impressive collection of Victorian-styled houses that for a while provided the city's most prestigious addresses. In 1885 a cable-car system, fashioned after San Francisco's, began serving an area west of downtown, and the 1,400 building lots plotted there by the system's owners. With advertisements that declared "Pure Air—No Fogs; Cheap lots

The expanding region was served by the expanding Pacific Electric rail system, which by 1914 stretched from San Bernardino to the Pacific Ocean. One of its more popular attractions was the line up Mt. Lowe, above Pasadena *(opposite top),* which featured an open car offering panoramic views of the valley below and the Pacific in the distance. Also popular was the downtown – Santa Monica line *(opposite bottom),* which ran through suburban Hollywood and the bean fields that were to become Beverly Hills and Westwood, to the beach. In the photograph, taken in the 1900s, a streetcar is making its run along Hollywood Boulevard, near Wilcox Street, in front of the Hurd residence. At right in the photograph is an early rendition of the system's eventual competitor and conqueror, the car.

in the Western Addition of the Cable Road," most were quickly sold. Service on the line collapsed almost as quickly. Another cable-car line, the Temple Street, serving yet more lots as far west as Alvarado Street was constructed, but it too ran into financial problems and, more critically, competition from the multiplying network of electric railways. In 1902 it was bought and closed down by Huntington, then on his way with funds from the sale of his interests in the oligarchical Southern Pacific to buying and melding L.A.'s fragmented transit systems, which he then expanded and improved. "We will join the region into one big family," declared Huntington, and for a time he did.

"Within a radius of 35 miles of Los Angeles, there are 42 incorporated cities and towns with countless country homes between," exclaimed an article in a 1913 issue of *Sunset Magazine.* "All these are literally of one body, of the healthiest and most rapidly growing body in America. The arterial system that holds them together is the double trackage of the interurban electric road. The red corpuscles that race to the end of every farthest vein to proclaim and carry the abundant life are the flitting crimson cars." The article also described the cars as "crimson chariots," declaring to the riders that they will "just wipe distance off the map, and your life shall be one long cocktail of orange blossoms, oceans, beaches, and Spring Street," Spring Street then being the heart of downtown.

What the system also created as it expanded farther and farther out was the suburban sprawl of Los Angeles that persists today. This is now served, not coincidentally, by a freeway network that generally follows the original routes of the interurban. More than a development pattern dictated by railways and realtors, the sprawl reflected a life-style consistent with the Southern California dream and sought by the millions of migrants leaving the industrializing and increasingly dense cities of the Midwest and East. While they might not be able to farm as they could have a few decades before, the newcomers could, because of mass transit and reasonable fares, "live in the country and work in the city," as a railway advertisement proclaimed in the early 1900s. It was a vision also supported at the time by various commentators and social philosophers.

"Instead of the pent-up millions in other cities, that from necessity or choice know only a contracted indoor existence, here will be found only healthy, happy families, scattered over a vast area," declared utopian reformer Dana Bartlett in *The Better City.* Author W. E. Smythe added in a 1910 article in *Out West* magazine that "a true Southern California city would be a garden filled with homes. Many of these homes would be humble, costing but a few hundred dollars, yet they would represent a very high average of beauty and comfort, thanks to the marvelous climate. In order to accommodate a great population, such cities would naturally spread over a vast area—the vaster the better." More bluntly, another social commentator of the times, G. Gordon Whitnall urged L.A. to be "not another New York, but a New Los Angeles. Not a great homogenous mass with a pyramiding of populations and squalor in a single center, but a federation of communities coordinated into a metropolis of sunlight and air." Here was to be a benevolent blending of the Garden City and City Beautiful movements that planners and utopians were promoting as answers to the ills of the industrial age.

Developers were quick to build on the image. No one was peddling just lots and houses, they were creating "garden commu-

70

nities," "fine suburbs," and "distinctive neighborhoods," all of them "just minutes to downtown" on the red car. And some, designed by the nation's most prestigious planning firms, were indeed distinctive, such as Palos Verdes Estates on the Palos Verdes peninsula.

The community was designed with extensive landscaping and parks, taking advantage of the peninsula's rolling terrain and views, by the firms of the Olmsted Brothers and Charles Cheney. The brothers were strong advocates of the City Beautiful movement founded in part by their father, Frederick Law Olmsted. The plan also called for limited commercial centers and a consistent, "Mediterranean" style overseen by a select architectural review board presided over by architect Myron Hunt. The hope was that the strict design controls would impress and attract the more affluent resident. It did, and the community today is one of L.A.'s more expensive and exclusive.

The red-car system not only served commuters and hauled freight, it was also used for recreation and tourism, playing an integral role in the daily life of the region during the boom years. "Groups frequently chartered private cars for Sunday-school picnics, singing trolley parties, and moonlight street-car excursions," recalled critic Franklin Walker in *A Literary History of Southern California.* "It was great fun to return from a weiner roast at Redondo on the Mermaid, poppies barely visible along the tracks in the moonlight, and youngsters out of the wicker seats in the open section in the back of the car, singing 'Down Went McGinty' and 'After the Ball.' One could always make the round trip to any of the beaches for fifty cents, and the famous daylong tours were not expensive. These rivaled the earlier Sante Fe Railway excursion trips on

'The Old Kite Route' which went from Los Angeles along the foothills to Redlands and back to Los Angeles via the Santa Ana Canyon and the Fullerton valley—'No scene twice seen on the kite-shaped track.' The Pacific Electric daily offered three 'specials': the Balloon Trip, a swing down to the beach at Santa Monica, then through the boom towns of Venice, Manhattan Beach, and Hermosa Beach, on to Redondo, and back by way of Culver City; the Old Mission Trip, which mixed orange trees and ostriches with Mission San Gabriel; and the Triangle Trip, down to Long Beach, Balboa, and Santa Ana, with glimpses of forest, of oil derricks, fields of sugar beets (the agricultural enthusiasm of the moment), and groves of almonds, lemons, and oranges. Best of all, there was the Orange Empire Excursion, run only twice a week, which took one to San Bernardino, Redlands, and Riverside. The high points of this expedition were the trip by Tally-Ho (a ranch) up to Smiley Heights near Redlands and the stop for lunch at Riverside Inn."

Even more critical to the growth of L.A. in the boom years was water. Indeed, water has been the basis of L.A.'s growth and prosperity since its founding. It was because the Los Angeles River flowed year round that the original pueblo had been located at its banks as an agricultural settlement. And because the pueblo, and eventually the city, controlled the water, it was able to expand, with nearby communities agreeing to annexation primarily in order to dip into L.A.'s supply. The supply in turn was fed by the sporadic rains and the runoffs from the surrounding mountains. Helping also were the natural below-ground reservoirs in valleys that would hold the runoffs, which were estimated as enough to sustain a thriving population of about 300,000. This was fine at the turn of the

century, when the city's population stood at about 100,000, but not enough in the minds of the boosters looking to the future with optimism and avariciousness.

"If you don't get the water, you won't need it," declared a taciturn William Mulholland, the city's water czar. Prompted by droughts in 1902 and 1903, the city took a series of steps to get that water by tapping the Owens Valley 250 miles to the north. Some of the steps were surreptitious, such as surveying the valley's water sources and purchasing select parcels there for the city, under the guise of a federal reclamation project; a few were suspect, such as the "flushing" of the existing supply in 1905, precipitating a water shortage just prior to a vote for a bond to plan an aqueduct from the Owens Valley to L.A.; and one was quite dramatic—building the actual aqueduct.

There were also hints of scandals, including the disclosure in 1905 that a syndicate, headed by Huntington and including a few of his banking and railroad associates, as well as the publishers of the *Times, Herald,* and *Express,* was quietly buying up large tracts of the then arid, and inexpensive, San Fernando Valley. The implication—eventually proven quite correct—was that when the water eventually came, land in the valley would be irrigated and naturally worth considerably more. If anything, the disclosure impressed the public, and the bond issue was approved by a margin of 14 to 1. The syndicate continued to buy land in the San Fernando Valley, and so did many others.

A subsequent bond issue in 1907 for funds to build the aqueduct was also overwhelmingly approved, as was the concept by then President Theodore Roosevelt. Responding to claims by Owens Valley farmers that L.A. was, in effect, raping their communities, Roosevelt declared that "it is a hundred or a thousand fold more important to the state that this [water] is more valuable to people as a whole if used by the city than if used by the people of the Owens Valley."

The construction of the aqueduct took five years and was one of the more impressive engineering feats in history, involving an estimated 5,000 workers, the boring of 142 tunnels, and the laying of 120 miles of railroad track and 500 miles of road to bring supplies to work crews. Mulholland was to make the speech at the dedication on November 5, 1913, turning over the aqueduct to the city. But, before he rose to speak, the gates of the last causeway were lifted, and the water began to flow, drawing the crowd away from the grandstand and toward the gushing aqueduct. Left without an audience, Mulholland is said to have turned to the mayor and declared, "There it is. Take it."

The city took the water and used it willfully in the following years to annex surrounding communities and serve an expanding population. By 1923 it was apparent that more than the Owens Valley supply would be needed, and the city turned to its next source, the Colorado. That effort would take fifteen years and include the construction of the Hoover Dam, as well as another, equally lengthy, aqueduct.

The boom years also were fed by a succession of oil strikes—creating jobs, generating wealth, and perpetuating the image of L.A. as a city of opportunity. Oil in the crude form of gurgling tar had actually been discovered in the region by the Spanish on the first overland expedition in 1769. In the following years, the tar was used for caulking ships and coating roofs, then as grease, and eventually as lamp oil. The first big strike came in 1892 when a maverick miner from Colorado, Edward Doheny, used his last few dollars to join with a

73

Spring Street in the 1920s was known as the "Wall Street of the West." Automobiles had begun to compete with the streetcars, and buildings with each other. This view is north from Seventh Street. The monumental clas-

sical structure, which hints of Moderne styling and projects an image of solidity, is the Pacific Stock Exchange, designed by Samuel Lunden, assisted by John and Donald Parkinson.

partner and sink a well a few blocks west of downtown at Glendale Boulevard and Second Street. A rich pool of oil was struck at 460 feet. Other wells and other strikes followed, and by 1900 the near northwest side was a forest of derricks, blessing residents with oil smells and splatterings, as well as sufficient royalties with which to buy or build a new house elsewhere.

That is exactly what many who struck oil did. Some of the more spectacular mansions of the day were built from oil profits, none more opulent than Doheny's Gothic-styled chateau in a Victorian oasis known as Chester Place, southwest of downtown. While the oil wealth had misshaped select sections of L.A., it certainly lent a style to others.

The strikes marched west, to the La Brea tar pits in 1902, the Fairfax district in 1904, and Beverly Hills in 1908. But while the supply of California crude steadily increased, the demand for its use as fuel wavered, causing prices to fluctuate sharply, bankrupting a few speculators, and, for a while during the teens, cooling the boom. But not for long.

The end of World War I saw a dramatic increase in the demand for oil, for new factories, homes, railroads switching from coal and, most of all, for automobiles. There was even a brief gas shortage in L.A. in 1919. With the timing of a good vaudeville trooper, and in the same spirit, wells indicating massive reserves blew in with a roar in 1920 in Huntington Beach, and in 1921 in Sante Fe Springs and Signal Hill. Others followed, and L.A. became "Oildorado," once again a rough-and-tumble frontier town, at least within smell of the oil. Tent cities on the edge of the oil fields blatantly offered gambling, prostitution, and liquor, though all three were illegal. The excesses kept pace with the oil strikes, which in turn tried to keep pace with the hype that the discoveries were generating.

Describing Sante Fe Springs after the big strike there, a genteel visitor declared that "it was just like a circus. They had big marquees with signs all over the place. There were gushers of oil spurting out, free lunches, men dressed in cutaway coats that would tell you: 'Invest a dollar and make a fortune.' "

Many invested, a few did make a fortune, but more were scalped. Some of the frauds were stupendous, such as the one involving Chauncey C. Julian and thousands of investors being taken for an estimated $150 million. The subsequent investigations and trials droned on, just like a bobbing pump in an oil field, drawing out at best a few drops a day. Various city politicians and boosters were implicated. Julian ran off to China, where he eventually committed suicide.

The booms and busts were beginning to change the character and social structure of L.A. "The people on the top in Los Angeles, the Big Men, are the business men, the Babbitts," observed acerbic journalist Louis Adamic in 1925. He described them as "the high priests" of the religion of "Climate and Profits," and added, "They are the promoters, who are blowing down the city's windpipe with all their might, hoping to inflate the place to the size that will be reckoned the largest city in the country . . . And trailing after the big boys is a mob of lesser fellows . . . thousands of minor realtors, boomers, promoters, contractors, agents, salesmen, bunko-men, officeholders, lawyers and preachers—all driven by the same motives of wealth, power, and personal glory . . . Then there are the Folks . . . they are the retired farmers, grocers, Ford agents, hardware merchants, and shoe merchants from the Middle West or wherever they used to live, and now they are here in California—sunny California—to rest and regain their vigor, enjoy the climate, look at pretty

scenery, live in little bungalows with a palm-tree or a banana plant in front, and eat in cafeterias." And perhaps strike it rich.

Among those who did literally strike it rich was Alphonzo Bell, who owned a modest house and two hundred acres in the heart of the Sante Fe Springs oil fields. With royalties bringing him up to $100,000 a month, Bell did not stay there very long. Following yet another gusher, this one catching fire within singeing distance of his house, Bell moved into the Beverly Hills Hotel. From there he surveyed a 2,000-acre tract of land west of the hotel and north of Westwood, which Bell felt had the potential of yet greater profits, not from oil but from housing sites. They were not just to be housing sites; they were to be estates. His wife named the tract BelAir. Bell's fortune ballooned.

Oil brought to L.A. more than just wealth, oil-field jobs, and the allure of gushing wells and get-rich schemes. It generated refining plants and fledgling research and development efforts, which in time were to grow into a thriving aviation and aerospace industry.

Movies were also bringing to L.A. wealth, jobs, and a certain flair. But instead of plants, there were studios, and instead of research and development, there was a fledgling entertainment industry. No longer were just tourism and health stimulating L.A.'s growth. Now it had industry—with a vengeance.

And while the water allowed L.A. to grow, the interurban gave it shape, and the oil spurred on the process, it was the movies that propelled it into the national consciousness and gave it a style. The style was Hollywood, a mix of reality and fantasy, often superficial and fleeting, taking a variety of forms, from architecture to eye makeup. And it turned L.A. into a dream town.

The Los Angeles Theater, located on South Broadway and designed in a fanciful French Renaissance style in 1931 by S. Charles Lee.

5
DREAM TOWN

Here, if anywhere else in America, I seem to hear the coming footsteps of the muse.

—William Butler Yeats, on a visit to L.A. in 1925.

In 1907, in search of mild weather, sunshine, and an ocean beach to complete the filming of a one-reel melodrama called *The Count of Monte Cristo,* the Selig Polyscope film company dispatched a director and a cameraman from Chicago to L.A. The pair liked what they saw, hired a few local actors, finished the film on time, and established a production office downtown. Word was soon filtering through the moviemaking community that L.A. lent itself well to filming. In addition to the good weather and light, L.A.'s broad beaches, dramatic seaside cliffs, rolling countryside, raw canyons, majestic mountains, deep forests, relaxed suburbs, and bustling city studded with an eclectic architecture, all provided a magnificent variety of sets and scenery for the fledgling filmmakers. For them L.A. was not a city, it was a sprawling studio.

L.A. also had the advantage, for some companies, of being out of the heavy-handed reach of the so-called Film Trust, then operating out of New York and trying to stifle competition by spurious lawsuits and nefarious sabotage. The distance to the West Coast tended to discourage the trust from dispatching subpoena servers and thugs.

The geographic area known as Hollywood remained relatively untouched in the first few years of filmmaking, as production companies galloped across the San Fernando Valley, cavorted on the beaches of Santa Monica, and disrupted traffic downtown. The area had been purchased by Horace and Daeida Wilcox in 1887, who as devout Methodists christened the land Hollywood and subdivided it with the vague hope that it would become a sort of genteel, bible-quoting suburb for those wanting to escape the hard-drinking, decadent life-style of downtown L.A. Saloons and the sale of liquor were banned

80

when Hollywood was incorporated as a city in 1903. A few years later, even movie theaters were banned, along with sanitariums, slaughterhouses, and oil wells. But, like other growing cities in the boom years of the 1900s, Hollywood needed water, and to get it from the Owens Valley Aqueduct, its sober citizenry agreed in 1910 to be annexed by L.A. Hollywood got water, but lost control over its future.

A year later the Nestor Film Company rented an empty saloon, at the corner of Sunset Boulevard and Gower Street, and converted it into a movie studio. Other film companies followed, among them the Jesse L. Lasky Feature Play Company. The company's production crew, headed by Cecil B. De Mille, had headed west from New York in 1913 to film *The Squaw Man* in Arizona, but when they arrived in Flagstaff they were greeted by a dust storm, cuing them to continue on to L.A. and, eventually, to Hollywood. The move to the then quiet suburb was prompted by the fact that production companies were being banned from filming in an increasing number of independent cities in the L.A. region, either with the tacit approval of the local police, or officially, as in Glendale, South Pasadena, and Santa Monica. It seems filming had become quite boisterous, turning streets into sprawling back lots, disrupting businesses and traffic. Annoying local communities, also, were the loose life-styles of actors, including those who, after a day filming westerns, would race their horses across lawns and through parks, while others in bars, restaurants, and rooming houses openly pursued more sybaritic endeavors.

God-fearing Hollywood residents protested, joining with a citywide group called Conscientious Citizens to gather some 10,000 signatures on petitions urging the L.A. City Council to ban moviemaking within the muni-

83

cipal limits, which now included Hollywood. But the petition was rejected, as the council noted that moviemaking was having an increasing impact on the economic life of the city, generating thousands of new jobs and stimulating reams of free publicity for the ever pro-growth region. By 1915, the film industry's annual payroll was estimated to be $20 million, and growing. The Lasky studio had burst out of the barn De Mille rented, to cover ten acres at the corner of Sunset and Vine, in addition to a rambling ranch in the San Fernando Valley. In the same year, to the cheers of 20,000 spectators, Carl Laemmle dedicated Universal City, a 230-acre studio, five miles north of Hollywood, where soon nearly a film a day was being produced.

A year later D.W. Griffith alone was employing 15,000 extras in his $2-million production of *Intolerance*, which included the construction of an enormous set depicting an ornate Babylon, replete with hanging gardens, at the corner of Sunset and Hollywood boulevards. During its brief life, the set became a tourist attraction, presaging the allure of studio tours decades later. Even the subsequent failure of the film at the box office, and World War I did not cause Hollywood to break stride, as the popularity of the movies swept the nation, prompting the production of more and more films and bigger and bigger studios. By 1920, some 100,000 Angelenos were employed in producing movies, which with a gross of an estimated $1 billion a year had become L.A.'s biggest industry, next to growth itself.

Indeed, the industry and Hollywood had become synonymous. Hollywood represented no longer just a residential and commercial center, but now a community in a socioeconomic sense, extending far beyond its physical boundaries. Hollywood, through the movies, in effect had become a state of mind, a myth, with profound consequences for L.A. and beyond. The movies had transformed Hollywood, and its neighboring communities of Beverly Hills and portions of L.A., into a dream town, sprinkled with the dream palaces of the stars.

Catapulted to wealth by the booming industry, the stars left the boardinghouses and rentals, which they had been plaguing with their parties and personalities, to build themselves homes. "In those days, the public wanted us to live like kings and queens," recalled Gloria Swanson in an interview. "So we did—and why not? We were in love with life. We were making more money than we ever dreamed existed, and there was no reason to believe it would ever stop." Having starred in De Mille's *Male and Female* in 1919, and *Why Change Your Wife?* in 1920, the then twenty-three-year-old Swanson bought a 22-room, 5-bath, Italian Renaissance mansion in

Whether not trusting their own success or not having much faith in the future of the industry, most in the fledgling film community in L.A. at first lived in rented quarters. One of the first to buy a home was Cecil B. De Mille *(below)* who in 1916 purchased a Spanish-styled estate in the Laughlin Park subdivision east of Hollywood. But it was Beverly Hills that, after being discovered by Fairbanks, became the favorite location for the "dream palaces" of the rich and famous. The subdued Italian Renaissance mansion *(opposite top)* was purchased by Gloria Swanson in the early 1920s. The neo-Gothic, Tudor Revival mansion *(opposite center)* was built in 1929 by oil magnate Edward Doheny for his son. A glimpse of Harold Lloyd's Greenacres *(opposite bottom)*, a 40-room, 26-bath extravaganza set in a sprawling hillside that included an 800-foot lake for canoeing, a golf course, and tennis and handball courts.

Beverly Hills. She then refurbished and re-decorated it with, among other extravagances, peacock silk, black marble, and a golden bath-tub, declaring that while a star, "I will be every inch and every moment a star." She had learned her cues well from De Mille.

The august De Mille had been the first member of the movie colony to buy a man-sion, paying $27,893, in 1916, for a Spanish-style estate in Hollywood's then exclusive Laughlin Park subdivision. Soon living nearby, in competitive splendor, were Charlie Chaplin and other stars of the day, but they had been content with buying the used mansions of oil and land barons. It was left to the king and queen of Hollywood, Douglas Fairbanks and Mary Pickford, to create their own palace and open up a new kingdom for development, Beverly Hills.

The community had been nothing much more than rolling fields of lima beans when it was bought by an oil syndicate in 1905 with the hope of finding rich deposits, like those discovered just to the east in what is now West Hollywood. Finding none, and having paid too much money for the land to just farm it, the syndicate decided to develop the area, not as another real estate subdivision but as a fashionable garden city. To design it, the syn-dicate hired Wilbur Cook, who had worked with the venerable Olmsted on the 1893 ex-position in Chicago, on the mall and the White House in Washington, D.C., and was considered one of the leading, land-use plan-ners of the period. Cook laid out a sensitive, balanced plan, calling for a range of housing types, from modest building sites south of what is now Wilshire Boulevard for shop-keepers and workers, to estates north of Sunset Boulevard. Plans were also drawn up for a commercial center and extensive landscaping and tree planting. To give the community an

Having generated reams of publicity using an Egyptian motif for a theater he built a few years earlier, film showman Sid Grauman selected a Chinese revival design theme for his most ambitious effort on Hollywood Boulevard. Architects Meyer and Holler gave Grauman a theater with an exterior in the form of a

Chinese temple *(opposite top)* and an interior resembling a Chinese palace. The forecourt was used for celebrity handprints, a tradition said to have been established when Norma Talmadge, touring the construction site with Grauman, slipped and fell hands first into some wet cement. Opened in 1927, the

Grauman's Chinese was the premier showcase for films during the halcyon days of Hollywood *(opposite bottom)*.
Below: To complement the French Renaissance exterior of his Los Angeles Theater, built in 1931, S. Charles Lee had the interior decorated in the style of the Hall of Mirrors of Versailles.

87

identity and to spur sales, the rambling, distinctive, Mission-style Beverly Hills Hotel was constructed and lushly landscaped. The hotel, completed in 1911, was a success, but land sales continued to be slow, despite the fact that members of the syndicate had built for themselves substantial, Tudor- and Spanish-styled mansions. Then, in 1919, Fairbanks bought a hunting lodge and fourteen acres on the top of Beverly Hills, changing the community forever.

Fairbanks promptly buried the lodge in an ambitious remodeling, creating a Tudor-styled mansion. He landscaped the grounds to include a huge swimming pool, a series of ponds for canoeing, a six-stall stable, and thousands of plantings. The transformation was a proper setting for his courtship of Pickford, even though "America's sweetheart" was at the time still married to Owen Moore. Within days after her divorce in March 1920, she and

Fairbanks were married; their estate was labeled Pickfair; and at last America had a royal couple.

Pickford and Fairbanks played the role well, entertaining celebrities and royalty from around the world, and turning Pickfair into a palace. Soon, if you were a star, Beverly Hills was the only place to be, and to build, and the bigger the better. Within a few years, residents included Will Rogers, Tom Mix, Charlie Chaplin, Rudolph Valentino, Pola Negri, Wallace Beery, John Barrymore, Buster Keaton, and Harold Lloyd, in a range and mix of neo-Spanish, Italian, Moorish, Georgian, and Tudor-styled mansions. In his social history, *Dream Palaces*, Charles Lockwood observed that "architectural purity was not an important consideration in Los Angeles at the time. Nor has it ever been. What really mattered in the 1920s was to achieve a romantic, faraway look, and most architects freely mixed different national, historic, and aesthetic styles on the same house to picturesque, often baffling effect."

One of the more ambitious estates built by a Hollywood personality was Lloyd's Greenacres. Designed in a rambling Spanish style by John de Lario, the thirty-six-thousand-square-foot house contained forty rooms and twenty-six bathrooms. There were also a nine-hole golf course and eight-hundred-foot-long canoe pond, no doubt in homage to Fairbanks.

The most extravagant house built in Beverly Hills in the 1920s, or anywhere else in L.A. before or since, was Edward Doheny's Greystone. After striking oil in the 1890s, Doheny had built one of the city's grand mansions on Chester Place, south of downtown, dabbled successfully in development, and eventually gained notoriety in the Teapot Dome scandal, in which it was revealed he

The Los Angeles City Hall *(opposite)* was designed in a modified Classical style by John C. Austin, Albert C. Martin, Sr., and John and Donald Parkinson, with Austin Whittlesey designing the interiors. It was the only structure for a half century allowed to exceed the city's 150-foot height limit, rising to twenty-eight stories. Completed in 1928, the form of the building, particularly the tower, resembles an earlier design by Bertram Goodhue of the Nebraska State Capitol. Goodhue was the architect for the Los Angeles Public Library *(below)*, completed in 1925. In the design can be seen various exotic styles being experimented with at the time, yet the clean lines of the stucture hint of modern forms to come.

gave a cabinet member a $100,000 bribe for secret leases to tap government oil reserves in California. Greystone was to be the Doheny castle. Designed by Reginald Johnson as a neo-Gothic, Tudor Revival mélange, the mansion totaled 46,504 square feet and dominated a 415-acre ranch, replete with a 15,666-square-foot stable, a seven-room gate house, two lakes, various swimming pools, numerous tennis and badminton courts, and extensive formal gardens. Its name was derived from the color and composition of the mansion's facade.

The elder Doheny never lived at Greystone but, instead, made a gift of it in 1929 to his only son, Edward, Jr. Three weeks after he moved in with his wife and five children, the son was shot dead in his bedroom by his male secretary, who then took his own life. Whether the shooting occurred during a quarrel over pay, the official version, or a lovers' quarrel, as many hinted, was never resolved.

However, it was absorbed into the myth and mysteries of Hollywood, then insinuating themselves in a variety of forms into L.A.'s life-style.

Architecture was a prominent form of the new life-style. Not content with just showing films, theaters in L.A. took on the look of opulent stage sets, right out of the films themselves. They were Egyptian and Mayan temples, Moorish mosques, Chinese pagodas, Spanish Baroque cathedrals, Renaissance palaces, and Romanesque palazzos, with lavish, ornamented, and furnished interiors. In the downtown theater district on South Broadway, architect S. Charles Lee recreated the lobby of the Paris opera house in the lobby of the Tower Theater, and a split-level, Versailles hall of mirrors in the Los Angeles Theater. Sparkling also in their ersatz exoticism on Hollywood Boulevard were, among others, the Pantages and Egyptian and Chinese theaters.

The palaces were pure escapism, designed as fantasies to help transport viewers into the make-believe world of films. Crowds flocked to films, and migrants, hopeful of stardom, or even just a job, flocked to Hollywood itself. Tourism was also booming. Thanks to the movies, the geographic community of Hollywood had grown from a population of about 4,000 in 1910, and 36,000 in 1920, to 150,000 in 1930. A quiet, suburban main street a few short years before, Hollywood Boulevard had become one of the most spectacular and glamorous streets in the world, "the Great White Way of the West."

The movie palaces were some of the more glittering examples of the expressive, exotic architecture seeded by Hollywood and beginning to sprout in the 1920s across the diverse L.A. landscape. In addition to the Mayan Theater, a downtown exuberance with cast-concrete ornamentation, designed by Morgan, Walls & Clements, there were Mayan-styled hotels, office buildings, and stores, and other pre-Columbian Revival conglomerations. The most accomplished composite of the period was the Los Angeles Public Library, designed by Bertram Goodhue and completed in 1926. With hints of Mediterranean, Roman, Islamic, Egyptian, and Byzantine styles, the library was topped by a marvelous, tiled pyramid. The total effect, replete with rich terracing to the south, was unique, a style unto itself. Damaged by a fire in 1986, it is to be renovated.

More mundane in its design, except for being allowed to exceed the city's 150-foot height limit and rise to 28 stories, was City Hall. A municipal monument with a touch of Romanesque in the classical, Beaux Arts tradition, it was completed in 1928, to become a set piece for film locations and political comedies. The rotunda appropriately resembles a movie-

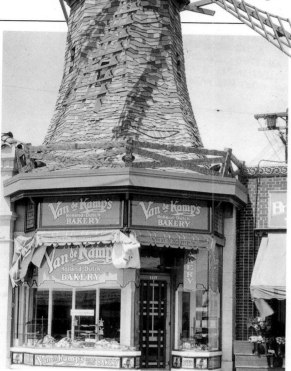

As commercial development became more oriented to the automobile, entrepreneurs looked for structures that could be easily identifiable and "read" from the road. The result was programmatic architecture, with cafés in the form of a pig, a dog, and an owl, among others. The owl was designed and built by its owner, Roy Hattrup, and had a head that rotated and eyes made from automobile headlights that actually blinked. There were also cafés designed in the form of their featured menu item, such as The Tamale, and shops whose design reflected their specialty, such as the windmill logo of the Van de Kamp's bakery, designed by Oliver.

When the firm of Morgan, Walls & Clements was commissioned to design a factory for the Samson Tyre and Rubber Company in 1929, it seemed reasonable that the architects would create a structure hinting of an Assyrian palace or a Babylonian wall. After all, those were the stomping grounds of Samson, for whom the company had been named.

92

palace lobby. More splendid was the Pasadena City Hall, along with the entire civic center. The orderly planning of the neo-Classical center was right out of the City Beautiful movement, while the design of City Hall, built in 1927, was an exotic Spanish Renaissance Revival. In the same style was the City Hall in Beverly Hills, right up to the top of its dome. It was completed in 1932, "during the Depression when people in this vicinity felt little pain," commented David Gebhard and Robert Winter in their guide to architecture in Los Angeles and Southern California.

Alert to the interest their stage sets had generated, various film companies had their offices designed in eclectic styles. There were English cottages, Southern plantations, and Roman forums. There was even a replica of Hansel and Gretel's cottage. Designed in 1921 by Henry Oliver, a set designer, to be used as the offices for Irwin C. Willat Productions in Culver City, the cottage had a sharply pitched, skewed roof and odd-shaped windows, and looked very much as if it had just jumped out of a book of fairy tales. It was an immediate hit and encouraged a more commercial use of expressive styles. Soon there was a Van de Kamp's Bakery designed as a windmill, a Hoot Hoot ice-cream parlor as an owl, a Brown Derby restaurant as a brown derby, a Chili Bowl restaurant as a chili bowl, a tamale stand as a tamale, and the Samson Tyre and Rubber Company as a Assyrian palace. The architecture proved to be a particularly effective form of advertising—three-dimensional billboards with a bang.

"If, when you went shopping, you found you could buy cakes in a windmill, ices in a gigantic cream can, flowers in a huge flower pot, you might begin to wonder whether you had not yet stepped through a looking glass or taken a toss down a rabbit burrow and could

expect Mad Hatter or White Queen to appear round the next corner. But there would be nothing unreal about it if you were in Hollywood, South California, for shops of that kind are to be seen in all of the shopping districts there," declared a 1938 edition of *The Modern Marvels Encyclopedia*, edited by John Crossland. Referring to these scenes on one of his sojourns here, Noel Coward is quoted as having said of L.A., "There is always something so delightfully real about what is phony here. And something so phony about what is real."

Also affected by the movies were various residential subdivisions. In L.A. researching his book *The American Jitters*, Edmund Wilson commented that numerous houses appeared to reflect the identity of the designers, builders, and owners, borrowing from "their favorite historical films, their best-loved movie actresses, their luckiest numerological combinations or their previous incarnations in old Greece, romantic Egypt, quaint Sussex or among the high priestesses of love of old India." As examples, Wilson cited "a Pekinese pagoda of fresh and crackly peanut butter," "a snow-white marshmallow igloo," "a toothsome pink nougat in the Florentine manner," "a clean pocket-size replica of heraldic Warwick Castle," "a wee wonderful Swiss shilly shally" and "a hot little hacienda, a regular enchilada con queso with a roof made of rich red tomato sauce."

It was the stuff of dreams.

Overleaf: The Academy Theater, a Streamline Moderne masterpiece designed by S. Charles Lee and built in 1939.

6

SHIFTING STYLES

I will open my own office in Los Angeles—which won't be so easy. I intend to build a small studio, and in case I get even a little work you can come over and help.

—From a letter by R.M. Schindler in L.A. to
Richard Neutra in Vienna, October 1921

While most architects and developers during the decades of feverish growth in L.A. played to the whims of buyers, with variations of Spanish Colonial, Italian Renaissance, English Tudor, French Chateau and other revivalist styles, or to their limited budgets with discounted versions of craftsman bungalows, a few notable designers were seeking more original forms. "The west has an opportunity unparalleled in the history of the world, for it is the newest white page turned for registration," declared Irving Gill in 1916. But Gill, who had worked briefly alongside Frank Lloyd Wright as a draftsman for Louis Sullivan in Chicago in the early 1890s, added that unfortunately the west "has been and is building too hastily, carelessly and thoughtlessly." If architects wanted to design buildings of note, Gill declared, they had to abandon distracting gimmicks and ornamentation, return to the basic forms of the straight line, the arch, the cube and the circle, and "dare be simple."

Gill certainly tried. After dabbling in the revival movement around the turn of the century, he experimented with a variety of structures, from modest, single-family houses and courtyard complexes to public buildings, developing a subtle, modern form. Gill's efforts, which paralleled the severe, international style then evolving in Europe, culminated in 1916 with the distinctive Dodge House. The house melded his concern for simplicity in exterior form and craftsmanship in interior detail. Though Gill continued experimenting, particularly in his design of the Horatio West Court complex in Santa Monica in 1919 and the Oceanside Civic Center in 1929, his practice waned in the wake of historical and exotic revivalism. But as Esther McCoy concludes in her classic *Five California Architects*, Gill very

The Barnsdall House *(below)* was the first of a series of commissions executed in L.A. by Frank Lloyd Wright. Designed for oil heiress Aline Barnsdall, the rambling wood-frame stucco house, completed in 1920, incorporated a flowing interior that had marked Wright's earlier Prairie School designs in the Midwest. But Wright, in an apparent effort to capture the flavor of the Southwest, wrapped the Barnsdall interior in a mock Mayan mass. Above the many and large windows, Wright placed a brow of stylized, cast-stone hollyhocks, the client's favorite flower, which lent the house its informal name, the Hollyhock House. While the house, with its high living room and Mayan mansard roof, looked heavy and forbidding, the interior *(bottom left)* was quite light and open, and, as in other Wright houses, focused on a monumental fire-

place. The house was part of a complex that included a spacious interior courtyard complete with fountain *(bottom center)* and a studio/guest house *(bottom right)*, designed by R. M. Schindler under Wright's supervision.

much left his mark on "that newest white page" to which he had been so attracted.

That page, and a lucrative commission, lured Frank Lloyd Wright to L.A. in 1917. The commission came from Aline Barnsdall, an eccentric oil heiress, who a few years before had left Chicago and a husband to indulge herself in the emerging social and cultural life of L.A. To mark her role, Barnsdall bought thirty-six acres on Olive Hill, a Hollywood landmark at what was then the suburban junction of Sunset Boulevard and Vermont Avenue. The crest of the hill was to be the site of her home, and the lower slopes a theater complex and an artists' colony. Wright was hired by Barnsdall on the basis of his earlier Prairie houses, which she admired. But while the interior of the house he designed for her followed the free-flowing, Prairie style, the exterior was a brooding Mayan-inspired mass. The resulting arguments between Wright and Barnsdall became legendary, with the heiress gaining the reputation as the architect's most difficult client ever. Eventually, Barnsdall moved into the house in 1921, along with her daughter, twelve dogs, and several servants. Perhaps not satisfied with the design, or concerned that the slovenly growth then overwhelming Hollywood had made the neighborhood déclassé, Barnsdall after a year abandoned the house, as well as the plans for the cultural center, leaving it all to the city as a park.

Meanwhile, Wright picked up a number of significant commissions in L.A., in which he continued his Mayan motif and expanded his experiments with a precast, concrete-block construction system. The commissions included the Millard and Storer houses in 1923, and the Freeman and Ennis houses in 1924, each one more imposing than the last, as if the stage-set syndrome, then insinuating itself

across the city, was also affecting Wright. Though intriguing, the so-called block system had structural problems and never caught on. Wright's son, Lloyd Wright, who after settling in L.A. to work for his father, embarked on his own distinguished career, designing a smattering of singular structures combining Mayan and Art-Deco styling, and eventually pioneering some striking modernist designs.

Also coming to L.A., under the wing of the elder Wright, to supervise construction of the Barnsdall house in 1920, was R.M. Schindler, a Viennese architect. After the project was completed, Schindler struck out on his own, designing for himself in West Hollywood in 1921 an exquisitely simple, sympathetic, modern house, a predecessor of much of his future work. In 1925, he designed the Lovell beach house on Balboa Peninsula,

a landmark of the International style, which was revolutionary for the time and place. Other, less severe, designs followed, as Schindler flowered as a domestic architect, his rationally conceived, ultimately reasonable houses gracing the city's sprawling foothills.

Just as Wright had enticed Schindler to L.A., Schindler in turn lured fellow-Austrian Richard Neutra. For a while in the mid 1920s the two worked together, but they soon fell out. As Norval White comments in *The Architecture Book*, Neutra was "an eastern European ego transplanted to the ego-land of Southern California." But, as White adds, Neutra also was "a towering talent," and this, combined with his ego, a flair for publicity, and a critical commission, soon put him at the head of the class championing modernism. The same Lovells for whom Schindler had designed the beach house now commissioned Neutra to design their city home. Again the Lovells wanted something distinctively modern, and they got it in a dramatic, steel-frame, prefabricated, paneled structure jutting out from a hillside like a monument to the dawn of the machine age. The house, bordering Griffith Park, was an instant hit when completed in 1929, attracting hordes of sightseers and generating for Neutra an international reputation and a thriving practice.

Among those who worked for, and learned from, Neutra were Harwell Hamilton Harris, Gregory Ain, and Raphael Soriano. They in turn went into practice for themselves in the 1930s, pushing the borders of modernism even further out with a variety of technically imaginative and sensitively executed structures. But while the works of these and other modernist architects produced some notable designs and lent L.A. a reputation as a testing ground of innovative architecture, historicism persisted.

"The eclectic procession to and fro in the rag-tag and cast-off of the ages is never going to stop," lamented Frank Lloyd Wright in 1934 in an attack on "Mexico-Spanish" styles in L.A. "The same thought, or lack of thought, was to be seen everywhere," he continued. " 'Taste,' the usual matter of ignorance, had moved toward simplicity a little, but thought or feeling for integrity had not entered into this architecture. All was flatulent or fraudulent with a cheap opulent taste for tawdry Spanish Medievalism." Observed critic Willard Motley, "It is the ambition of every citizen of L.A. to have a palm tree in his front yard and two citrus trees in his backyard. Add an atrocious glorified-barn structure called a house, stuccoed and white-washed and weighted down by red or green tiles, and the 'native son' is a happy man in a God-ordained, man-made paradise."

While modernists derided the "stucco rash," the public seemed to love it. The style decorated almost every structure conceivable, from houses, stores, and gasoline stations to mortuaries, banks, and city halls. One of its more charming uses was for apartment courts. An outgrowth of the previously popular, modest, bungalow courts, the more ambitious apartment courts usually went to two stories and expressed Mediterranean themes with hand-painted tiles, fountains, and lush landscaping, in addition to the white stucco walls and red-tile roofs. Among the more opulent were a series of complexes designed by Arthur and Nina Zwebell in the 1920s, which became models for less imaginative efforts in the 1930s.

With their common areas encouraging neighborly mingling, the apartment courts made pleasant enclaves in a city that in the crush of growth was becoming increasingly anonymous and alienating. Word about them was spread by letters sent home to guide others

103

coming to L.A., and through friends and colleagues in the city. Particular apartment courts became identified with particular hometowns, acting troups, political movements, social groups, and other loose associations. Select courts in effect became neighborhoods with a sense of place and community, satisfying a recurring dream of generations of settlers in L.A.

That dream had at times, in the growth of the L.A. region, stimulated a host of social experiments, including the establishment of various, utopian planned communities. Among cities in the region that got their start as such communities were Pasadena (farmers from Indiana forming an agricultural cooperative), San Bernardino (Mormon settlers), Anaheim (German vintners), and El Toro (English immigrants). Communities were also formed by political refugees, social reformers, extended families, religious groups, professional colleagues, and enlightened developers. One of the more visionary was a socialist cooperative known as Llano del Rio embracing 10,000 acres in the Antelope Valley in the 1910s. At its height the cooperative had 1,000 residents, a school, library, and symphony orchestra, before succumbing in 1918 to internal and external political pressures, and financial problems.

From a design point of view, the most ambitious planned community in the 1930s was Baldwin Hills Village, also known as Village Green, a 627-unit apartment complex shaped by a team that included planners Reginald Johnson and Clarence Stein, the architectural firm of Wilson, Merrill & Alexander, and landscapers Fred Barlow and Fred Edmondson. The village was designed with all the roads and garages confined to the edges of its eighty-acre expanse. This border created a park in which apartments were clustered in a

While working for Frank Lloyd Wright as the supervising architect on the Barnsdall House, R. M. Schindler designed a simple, small house for himself, his practice, and a friend on Kings Road in West Hollywood *(below)*. The straightforward post-and-beam, curtain-walled structure marked the quiet introduction into L.A. of the International style. Though the style was severe, the siting and flow of interior space into a courtyard *(bottom left)* showed a sensitivity to the local conditions and life-styles. This sensitivity was demonstrated well in the Elliott House *(bottom right)*, an open, airy, well-detailed modern design in Los Feliz, constructed in 1931.

In the Falk Apartments *(below)*, built in 1939 on a steep incline in Silver Lake, Schindler turned the structure and stacked the units so that each unit would have a terrace and a view, and encouraged landscaping. The apartment complex marked Schindler's more relaxed embrace of the severe International style he had exercised with rigor 14 years earlier in his design for the Lovell beach house on Balboa Peninsula *(bottom)*.

The Lovell House *(below)*, designed by Richard Neutra in 1929, established L.A. as a prime testing ground for the International style and the Modern movement. With an all-steel frame construction, strong horizontal lines, and extensive use of glass, the house, cantilivered above a canyon in Los Feliz at the edge of Griffith Park, presented the image of a formal institution. Yet its light, airy interior, enhanced by an open plan, was quite informal. Encouraged by the interest in the house, Neutra continued to explore the style in numerous commissions in L.A. He also designed a house for his growing family and growing practice, calling it the V.D.L. Research House *(opposite)*, in recognition of a grant he received from an appreciative businessman, C. H. Van Der

series of garden courts, each a distinct neighborhood. "The idea was that without cars zooming past your front yard, and common green areas instead of streets, it would be safer and people would get to know their neighborhoods a little better, and create a communal feeling," explained Estelle Leroy, who with her husband Ben has lived in the village for thirty years.

The village was a recognition that the automobile was becoming a major determinant in the shaping of the L.A. landscape. A short drive north of Baldwin Hills, a section of Wilshire Boulevard known as the Miracle Mile was flourishing as the city's prime retail district. It had been assembled and developed in the late 1920s and early 1930s with the car

very much in mind. "The first real monument of the Motor Age," declared historian Reyner Banham in his *Los Angeles: The Architecture of Four Ecologies*. Stores were designed to catch the eye of passing motorists and rear parking lots provided. Other shopping districts catering to the car also began taking form, such as Westwood Village. They were being prompted by the dispersal of housing subdivisions, farther and farther away from the interurban system, which made residents more and more dependent on the private car. New and native Angelenos did not recoil, but rather embraced the new form of transportation.

Soon after reasonably priced cars started to roll off the assembly lines in the 1910s, L.A. had more cars per citizen than any other city

The Andalusia Apartments in West Hollywood was one of a series of exotic housing complexes developed by Arthur and Nina Zwebell in the 1920s. Built in 1929, the Andalusia was the Zwebells' most ambitious and fanciful project. It was designed in a romantic Spanish Revival style and featured duplex apartments. The complex includes a forecourt for cars *(bottom)* and a central court for residents *(right)*, decorated with hand-painted tiles and lushly landscaped.

Though attractive, apartment complexes such as the Andalusia were not particularly affordable, especially in the 1930s. How to design affordable complexes that were also attractive and took advantage of L.A.'s climate and landscape was a constant challenge to the architects of the day. One of the more successful designs in this period was Dunsmuir Flats just west of the Crenshaw district. The architect was Gregory Ain, who had worked for Richard Neutra from 1931 to 1935 before establishing his own practice and, in time, his own reputation as a socially conscious architect of the Modern movement. Built in 1939, the project consisted of four two-story units gracefully sited on a 49-foot-wide lot (*below*). Though the north façade was a closed arrangement of connected cubes, the south façade (*bottom*) displayed an open, informal plan overlooking private gardens.

The most ambitious planned apartment complex of the time was Baldwin Hills Village, also known as Village Green. Developed in the late 1930s and confining vehicular traffic and parking to the perimeter of the site, a central "village green" was created. The project was designed by planners Reginald Johnson and Clarence Stein, of the architectural firm Wilson, Merrill and Alexander, and landscape architects Fred Barlow and Fred Edmondson.

in the country. While L.A. County's population was doubling from 750,000 to 1.5 million from 1915 to 1924, auto registration rose eightfold, from 55,217 to 441,000. Most of the migrants flocking to L.A. in the following years came by automobile. L.A. had become a "motorized civilization," a model for human adaptation to the automobile.

Climate was a factor, for open and unheated cars could be used year-round, and the inviting landscape helped too. But more than anything else, it was the liberating independence the car provided to its driver which complemented L.A.'s promise of easy access to the good life. Visiting L.A. in 1923, author Sir Arthur Conan Doyle took a pleasure drive, joining what seemed to him an endless parade of automobiles. "When we crowned a hill and looked back we could see the whole long road dotted thickly, even when we were fifty miles from the city, for it was Sunday and everyone was out. There were no bicyclists and no pedestrians." Inexorably, the interurban transit system began to suffer, while the area's roadways were expanded and improved. The concept of limited-access highways gained increasing support, and by 1939 L.A. had its first freeway, the Arroyo Seco Parkway, later renamed the Pasadena Freeway, running six miles from downtown L.A. to Pasadena.

Reflecting L.A.'s love of the car and motion, the Streamline Moderne architectural style of the 1930s was characterized by horizontal lines, rounded corners, projecting wings, and generally a sleek, machine-like look which expressed efficiency and modernity. It was the "smart" style, and it was applied to everything from ashtrays and radio sets to cars and locomotives. But most of all it was applied to buildings, including a rich display of stores and shops along Wilshire Boulevard, the Coca-Cola bottling plant downtown, the

central post office, city hall and the Shangri-La Hotel in Santa Monica, and a variety of commercial structures and apartment complexes throughout L.A.

The style was a marriage of convenience between the Modern and Art Deco movements. Also labeled Zigzag Moderne, Art Deco had been inspired in part by a provocative decorative and industrial arts exhibit in Paris in 1925. Architects quickly used its stylized themes to lend verve and individuality to the more formal Beaux Arts style. The results were some stunning structures, which glowed with the imaginative application of highly glazed, colorful terra-cotta and soared skywards in grand architectural gestures exuding prosperity and confidence. Among the many magnificent buildings produced in this brief but shining period of L.A. architecture was the elegant Bullock's Wilshire department store, the nearby Pellissier Building and adjacent Wiltern Theater, the Sunset Tower apartments, and downtown the Garfield and Eastern Columbia buildings.

What pared down Art Deco into the more subdued Streamline Moderne style were not only the growing influence of the severe International movement and the machine aesthetic, but also the Depression. It was not a time to display the wealth of Art Deco, even if developers then could afford it, which few could. The more modest Streamline Moderne

Two of L.A.'s grand passions, cars and movies, were wedded in the early 1930s in a drive-in theater on Pico Boulevard, claiming to be "California's First" *(below).* Increasingly, the car was asserting itself in competition with the Pacific Electric streetcar system as the region's prime means of transportation, with occasional disastrous results *(bottom).* The accident was in Cahuenga Pass near the Hollywood Knolls subdivision, as the sign indicates.

Below: The 1930s began with the Curtis Wright Flying Service maintenance building being the only structure at a municipal airport that was not much more than a dirt runway and a few wooden shacks located in a for-

mer beanfield near the ocean. Dedicated as Hanger No. 1, it was designed in a not particularly expressive Spanish Colonial Revival style by the architectural firm of

Gable and Wyant. But the aircraft that were being designed in L.A. and worked on in this hangar and others were indeed expressive, and paced the local aircraft industry to rank number one in the nation by the end of the decade.

style seemed more appropriate, and certainly was less expensive to build. And build they must, for despite the Depression, L.A. continued to grow. But the growth took on a different flavor. L.A.'s earlier image of the land of sunshine and oranges, opportunity and prosperity, faded in the deepening shadows of the 1930s. Along with the shifts in L.A.'s architectural styles were some subtle, and not so subtle, shifts in cultural styles.

Actually, these changes had been brewing for some time, but only became more apparent during the Depression. The shift had been touched off in part by the popularity of the movies, which in the 1920s, according to social commentator Carey McWilliams, began to attract to L.A. all sorts of odd types: "dwarfs, pygmies, one-eyed sailors, showpeople, misfits, and 50,000 wonder-struck girls," followed by "pimps, gamblers, racketeers and confidence men." Added local critic Louis Adamic in *Laughing in the Jungle,* "In spite of the healthful sunshine and ocean breezes," L.A. was "a bad place—full of old, dying people, and young people who were born of tired pioneer parents, victims of America—full of curious wild and poisonous growths, decadent religions and cults of fake science, and wild-

Streamline Moderne and its hints of a modern age became the "smart" style in L.A. in the late 1930s. When the Coca-Cola company decided to remodel a bottling plant south of downtown, it had Robert Derrah design the structure as a sleek ocean liner *(below)*. Included were a ship's bridge, a promenade deck, portholes, and various nautical detailing, lending the plant the clean image the company was then seeking. The Shangri-La Hotel in Santa Monica (*bottom*), designed by

Previous pages: The Pan-Pacific Auditorium in the Fairfax district was, when it opened in 1935 to host an auto show, an appropriately slick statement of Streamline Moderne. With its four flagpole pylons shaped like giant fins, the sculpted façade hinted of speed and energy and reflected the public's fascination with the machine aesthetic. Actually, the design by William Wurdeman and Welton Becket was little more than a façade on a barn of a building, though as a symbol the façade was quite impressive, and effective.

William Foster, turned the corner of Ocean and Arizona avenues with élan. As designed by S. Charles Lee, the Academy Theater on Manchester Boulevard in Inglewood (*seen below from the rear*) incorporated nearly all of this style's favored detailing, including harmonizing curved walls and glass brick, topped by a thin, cylindrical tower wrapped with a molding spiraling up to meet a spherical sunburst.

Completed in 1939, Union Station was the last of the nation's great railroad passenger terminals to be built. Trying to be regional yet modern, the design is a subdued Spanish Colonial Revival, with touches of Streamline Moderne. The architectural team included John and Donald Parkinson, J. J. Christie, H. L. Gilman, and R. J. Wirth. The landscaping by Tommy Tomson featured two courtyards of lush, fragrant plantings.

cat business enterprises, which, with their aim at quick profits, were doomed to collapse and drag down multitudes of people."

Prohibition did not help. Being near Mexico, where the production of liquor was legal, and with a varied and extensive coastline well-suited to smuggling, L.A. became one of the bootleg capitals of the country, and one of its "wettest" cities. There were also drinking and gambling ships anchored in the Pacific out of the reach of local authorities, which created the situations and characters Raymond Chandler captured in his novel *Farewell, My Lovely*. Scandals involving the police and politicians were periodically uncovered, followed by resignations, impeachments, sensationalized trials, an occasional murder, and other municipal mayhem. Adding to the chaos were bloody Tong wars ripping apart Chinatown.

Lending the crime and corruption a desperate air was the fact that Hollywood seemed to mock and mimic the Depression in its movies and lifestyles. The resulting scenes fed the imaginations of writers like Chandler, Nathanael West, Evelyn Waugh, Aldous Huxley, and James Cain. With varying degrees of satire and sting, they depicted L.A. in the 1930s as a city of disillusionment and destruction, a sinister place where, in the deepening shadows of despair, lurked an evil that only some sort of apocalypse could cleanse. For them the hope L.A. had engendered for generations with its myths of prosperity and happiness had collapsed in frustration and fakery into a harsh anti-myth.

Reflecting on this L.A. with a painter's eye was West's protagonist Tod Hackett in *The Day of the Locust* as he walked home one evening to his house in the Hollywood Hills:

The edges of the trees burned with a pale violet light and their centres gradually turned from deep purple to black. The same violet piping, like a Neon tube, outlined the tops of the ugly, humpbacked hills and they were almost beautiful. But not even the soft wash of dusk could help the houses. Only dynamite would be of any use against the Mexican ranch houses, Samoan huts, Mediterranean villas, Egyptian and Japanese temples, Swiss chalets, Tudor cottages, and every possible combination of these styles that lined the slopes of the canyon.

When he noticed that they were all of plaster, lath, and paper, he was charitable and blamed their shape on the materials used . . . plaster and paper know no law, not even that of gravity.

On the corner of La Huerta Road was a miniature Rhine castle with tarpaper turrets pierced for archers. Next to it was a highly coloured shack with domes and minarets out of the Arabian Nights. Again he was charitable. Both houses were comic, but he didn't laugh. Their desire to startle was so eager and guileless. It is hard to laugh at the need for beauty and romance, no matter how tasteless, even horrible, the results of that need are. But it is easy to sigh.

Coloring the vision of writers and commentators were some very real catastrophes. In addition to the Depression, there was the collapse in 1928 of the St. Francisquito Dam, which killed 400 people. An earthquake centered in Long Beach in 1933 killed 120 and caused $40 million of damage. This was followed in 1934 by a disastrous flood, a freak frost in 1937 that destroyed half the region's citrus crop, and more floods in 1938. There also were bloody strikes, record bankruptcies, and political shenanigans, in particular the use of scare tactics to defeat Upton Sinclair's populist bid for governor in 1934. Other nefarious acts of the period had the L.A. police patroling the state line, and in violation of basic civil liberties, turning back migrants who looked less than prosperous.

Yet the migrants still came, for, as one said, he might starve in L.A., but he wouldn't freeze. The city was hurting, though not as

125

bad as others. Its pride and public works were given a boost by the 1932 Olympics, which (like the 1984 Olympics) produced a profit for the city. Hollywood continued to prosper, its films providing the great escape through fantasies for a struggling nation, while its stars achieved the status of aristocracy. And while the "odd" types continued to flock to Hollywood, so did "an unprecedented and unrepeatable population of genius, neurosis, skill, charlatanry, beauty, vice, talent, and plain old eccentricity," according to Reyner Banham in his architectural history of L.A. And Banham added that the lure of Hollywood "brought that population in little over two decades, not the long centuries that most metropolitan cities have required to accumulate a cultured and leisured class."

Meanwhile, agricultural and oil production held steady, though not without labor problems, stimulating equipment and research companies. Jobs also were being generated by the construction of another aqueduct, this one tapping the Colorado River, where the Boulder Dam was rising to provide needed electrical power for L.A. As the threat of war heightened in Europe and in Asia, the city's young aircraft industry grew to rank first in the nation. And when war came, L.A.'s industries boomed, attracting an eager migrant work force, impressing the millions of troops passing through the city, and setting the stage for new growth.

Overleaf: Case Study House #22; Pierre Koenig, architect.

7

THE ROARING 50s

*As the 1940s ended, people were pouring in at the rate of 3,000 a week, look-
ing for a roof, a job and a place to park. The sun above the beaches, parks and
boulevards they had seen so often on the screen was obscured at times by a
sepia ceiling that stung their eyes, but on a clear day they could still see
Catalina and, perhaps, Mickey Rooney. Overnight they became Angelenos.*

—John D. Weaver, *California History*, Volume LX

The war matured L.A. No longer the
gangly, awkward star-struck youngster of
the 1920s, or the troubled, searching adolescent of the 1930s, it exuded the confidence of
a young industrial power. The federal government had poured billions of dollars into the
city as part of the war effort, laying the foundation for a new prosperity after the war,
which was paced by the evolution of aircraft manufacturing into the aerospace industry.
Also booming were the oil industry and allied endeavors, like the plastics business, which
generated, among other things, hula hoops. Everything in L.A. seemed to be coming up
roses, cultivated by the pent-up capital and dreams of World War II. Success bred success,
attracting new waves of migrants, an estimated one million in the immediate postwar
years and two million more in the roaring 1950s, bringing the population of the L.A.
region to about six million in 1960. With their roots loosened in the war, vision broad-
ened by travel, and education strengthened by the G.I. bill, these latest migrants were full
of hope, looking for a place where they could enjoy the promise of an America they had
fought for, a glimpse of the future, a place in the sun.

L.A. "suddenly was more than flowers, winter vegetables, oranges, movies, and oil der-ricks," recalled local observer and social historian Richard Lilliard. "The war, which was as Asian as European, and a holocaust in the Pacific, had made Los Angeles the premier West Coast port for ships and planes. It handled more seaport tonnage than San Fran-cisco, landed more fish than Boston and Gloucester, and together with satellite cities it made more planes than any other metropolis on earth. Los Angeles also assembled more

129

cars than any city but Detroit, baked more tires than any city but Akron, made more furniture than Grand Rapids, and stitched together more clothes than any city except New York—and even led New York in designing and manufacturing sportswear." And this on top of its continued lead as the nation's entertainment capital. But now, in addition to grinding out movies and radio programs, there were productions for an emerging television industry. All eyes were on L.A., which through programs like "Ozzie and Harriet" and "Leave It to Beaver" created the "mythology" of a suburban life-style for which Americans yearned.

To house the region's burgeoning population, down went the orange trees and up went the tract developments, in what was to be the longest, continuous real estate boom in L.A.'s history. Building sprawled west across the San Fernando Valley, east into the San Gabriel Valley and south, spilling over into Orange County, just as had been predicted and mapped in various regional-planning studies in the 1940s. While downtown L.A. was still to be the major center of the region, the plans called for a variety of lesser commercial and industrial centers which would provide jobs and services for neighborhoods of mostly single-family homes. The garden city prevailed: that is what the returning veterans seemed to want and that was what L.A. was determined to offer.

Gobbling up farmland, cropping mountains, and scarring hillsides to spew out so-called "off the rack" houses were hundreds of enterprising builders, of whom Louis Boyar emerged as the most ambitious. Purchasing 3,375 acres in 1950, Boyar laid out Lakewood Park, a community of 17,000 homes for a population of 70,000 persons. Twice the size of the more publicized Levittown then rising in

Most housing developments in the 1950s marched unimaginatively over the L.A. landscape, providing shelter but little else (*opposite top*). The developers of Crestwood Hills in Kenter Canyon in Brentwood tried to be different. They began the develop-ment as a cooperative, hired an imaginative design team to devise an environmentally sensitive land-use plan, set aside select sites for community facilities, and encouraged innovative housing schemes. The design team included Whitney Smith, Edgardo Contini, and A. Quincy Jones. Jones also designed a number of attractive modest, modern, and, above all, functional houses in the Crestwood development (*below and opposite bottom*).

the East on Long Island, Lakewood became a prototype of mass-produced housing.

"While the farmers were harvesting the last crop from the land, Boyar's construction crews were starting to lay 133 miles of paved streets," observed Remi Nadeau in his history *Los Angeles from Mission to Modern City*. "Small teams of specialists moved down one side of each street with fantastic new machinery. Great power diggers gouged out a foundation trench for a house in 15 minutes. Lumber arrived precut for each home. Conveyor belts carried shingles to the roofs. Carpenters used automatic nailing machines and powered door-hanging machines. Expediters with radio cars moved from one home to another looking for bottlenecks. On some days as many as 100 new homes were started; 10,000 were finished in the first two years. Mass construction was matched by mass sales; by late 1950 the volume reached 107 sales in a single hour."

Though the tract houses provided shelter and, to an extent, fulfilled the dream of an affordable single-family house, most of the developments were marked by insensitive planning and undistinguished designs. It was a situation that a group of L.A.'s more visionary and social-minded architects had feared. As members of a jury judging a competition in 1945 sponsored by the U.S. Plywood Corporation for a "$5000 to $6000 house for the average American workman," they had declared in a report that if architects did not address then the problem of providing well-designed housing in well-planned subdivisions for the expected flood of families in the postwar years, "it will be badly solved later by the jerry builders." The report, written in large part by architect and urban planner Gregory Ain, concluded that "too many architects in their zeal to promulgate new and frequently valid ideas withdraw from the common archi-

131

The Case Study House program, which ran from 1945 to 1962, showcased how the International style and the latest construction materials and methods might be adapted to the relaxed life-style of L.A. Among the more notable houses developed was #22 *(be-* *low)*, designed by Pierre Koenig in 1959. It demonstrated the benefits, and the drama, of using steel columns and beams, and allowed three sides of the structure to be clad in glass nonbearing walls. The result was a 240-degree view of L.A. The house was somewhat more luxurious in its space and setting than Koenig's earlier spartan Case Study House #21 *(opposite)*. Unlike #22, which was built on the edge of a precipice, #21 was built on a level site. The house consisted of a series of 10' x 22'

tectural problems of the common people." Ain, in time, proved to be an exception.

The competition had been conducted by *Arts & Architecture* magazine, a crusading and innovative professional journal then under the dedicated editorial direction of John Entenza. According to architectural historian Esther McCoy, the magazine during the 1940s "was the picture of a period with a strong social conscience, a reflection of the idealism and puritanism of the Depression and the war years when architecture was first of all a social art." It was out of this "fine prejudice," she added, that the so-called Case Study House program emerged, heralding what was perhaps L.A. architecture's finest hour. The program was conceived by Entenza to illustrate how modern design might meet the need for both affordable and attractive postwar housing. "It

did not encourage heroics; what it asked for was service," declared McCoy in the introduction to a monograph on the program.

With the magazine acting as client, sites were purchased and architects commissioned, among them, over the years Richard Neutra, Eero Saarinen, Charles Eames, Craig Ellwood, J.R. Davidson, Raphael Soriano, Pierre Koenig, Whitney Smith, and A. Quincy Jones. The resulting houses pioneered a host of structural and design concepts, garnered numerous awards, attracted international attention, reinforced L.A.'s reputation for innovative architecture, and generated considerable builder and buyer interest. The first six houses completed in the first three years alone were visited by 368,554 persons. Eventually twenty-eight houses were completed, most during the 1950s, and their designs inspired a

133

One of the first houses assigned to be designed and built under the Case Study program in the late 1940s was the Eames House *(left)* in Santa Monica Canyon. The steel frame, glass-and-panel structure was designed by Charles Eames in the form of a bridge and incorporated a house and a studio for Eames and his wife, Ray. They are seen together *(below)* in the living room of the house.

general acceptance of the modern motif and its commitment to a relaxed living environment appropriate to L.A.

During this time there also were a number of efforts to develop more environmentally and socially conscious housing tracts. A leading figure in this effort was Gregory Ain, who, in his youth, lived for a year in Llano del Rio, a socialist-inspired cooperative that for a brief period flourished in the Antelope Valley north of L.A., and later, as an architect, was impressed by the sensitively planned Baldwin Hills Village.

With Simon Eisner as planner and Garrett Eckbo as landscape architect, Ain pursued the development of a 280-unit cooperative on a hundred acres in the San Fernando Valley community of Reseda. The project, called Community Homes, was to be a model neighborhood, sensitively landscaped with parks, playgrounds, and plantings. But after years of planning the Federal Housing Administration denied the project financing. It seems some of the potential homeowners were racial minorities. This was a violation of something called Regulation X which, out of the fear that resale values would be harmed, prohibited federal funding for projects where there was a mixing of races. There were strong protests in which it was noted that many of the subscribers in question were veterans who had fought in the war. All was in vain, and the plans were scrapped, with the land eventually falling into the hands of so-called "down-and-dirty" developers. Architectural historian Esther McCoy commented in her chapter on Ain in *The Second Generation*, "Five years after Community Homes was disbanded and the property sold, Reseda was the lowest common denominator of tract housing—no green belts or finger parks, just houses set row on row as exactly as markers in a VA cemetery. In the cemetery, however, there was no Regulation X."

Some of Ain's imaginative plans were developed, in Silver Lake and, in particular, in Mar Vista. But even there the FHA haunted him, reducing the number of units it would finance and requesting that, in the interest of "good business practice," ranch and saltbox designs be mixed with his modern schemes.

Another innovative effort was Crestwood Hills in Kenter Canyon in Brentwood. Crestwood was conceived by four musicians who were friends and thought it would be nice if they could get a piece of land and build their houses near one another, and maybe a couple more houses, too. So did a few hundred other people who responded to an advertisement the

musicians placed in the *Los Angeles Times* in 1946, to see if anyone else would be interested in joining them and putting down $25 each toward the effort. The result was a cooperative, known as the Mutual Housing Association, which, after selecting a tract of land, hired an architectural and engineering team to come up with a land-use plan and some prototype housing designs. The team of A. Quincy Jones, Whitney Smith, and Edgardo Contini did that and more, setting aside select sites for a community center, park, nursery school, and outdoor theater. It also laid out roads so they followed the contours of the canyon, twisting and turning, and rising and falling, and therefore minimizing bulldozing and damage to the verdant landscape and views.

The same care went into the placement of the houses, making sure they did not block the views of neighbors. It was an environmentally sensitive plan at a time when there were few such concerns. Though the cooperative fell victim to the deadly combination of Regulation X and financial problems, the planning concept survived, to be developed, at least in part, into one of the city's more attractive communities.

Becoming more popular in this period was the California ranch house, a distinctly regional creation that grew out of the earlier adobe rancho and later bungalow styles, borrowed some modern elements and combined them with imagination and frugality, depending on builders and budgets, so it could fit

The Modern style championed in the Case Study program was widely adapted with much popular success to the less severe Ranch House style. *Opposite:* The Wilcox House in Pasadena was designed by the firm of Whitney Smith and Wayne Williams in 1956. *Below:* The Cliff May House was considered the ultimate ranch house. It was May, more than any other designer or developer in the 1950s, who perfected the rambling informality of the California Ranch House. No date could be put on the house in Sullivan Canyon in Brentwood because May constantly redesigned, reconstructed, and renovated it as part of a continuing design experiment.

Below: The Avenel Cooperative, designed by Gregory Ain. As he had before the war, Ain once again was trying to use the modern motif to overcome a tight site on a steep slope and create an apartment complex at a reasonable cost. This one in Silver Lake was designed for ten families, most of them members of a cartoonists' union. Ain's most ambitious postwar project was a plan for 100 houses on a 60-acre site west of Culver City, to be known as Mar Vista. Ain designed all the houses in a Modern style (*bottom*). But the federal agency involved in financing the development required that the designs include Ranch and Salt Box styles to aid marketing. And when the project, reduced to 52 houses, did not sell well at first, the agency blamed the poor sales on the Modern styles. If Ain's designs were considered risky, Bernard Judge's were even more so. His Bubble House (*opposite*), built atop Beachwood Canyon in the late 1950s, attracted much attention, but could not withstand the elements and the vandals.

Most apartments built in the 1950s were little more than stucco boxes. Since their style was often tacked on in the form of modish lettering and ornamentation (*below*), they were frequently derided as "dingbats."

Yet they did provide shelter for the millions flocking to L.A. and remain, like their more sensitively sited and less dense antecedent, the bungalow court, a popular and populist form of housing.

The stack *(opposite)*. Completed in 1953, the downtown interchange connects the Harbor-Pasadena and Hollywood-Santa Ana freeways and became a symbol of the emerging auto-oriented city.

142

The California coffee shop in the 1950s took Modernism one step beyond, giving it wings, angles, texture, color, and just about anything else that would catch the eye and lure a passing motorist to the plastic interiors. Designs included the soaring ''A'' frame of Coffee Dan's in Van Nuys (*below*), hinting of Polynesia, designed by the firm of Palmer & Krisel. Angles were emphasized, and wherever possible, walls, roofs, and interiors were slanted and stylized (*bottom*).

The coffee shop style peculiar to the 1950s was labeled "Googie," after the name of a West Hollywood restaurant designed with a flair by John Lautner. The style was embraced and expanded upon by the firm of Armet & Davis, which designed buildings for various L.A. chains, including Norm's, Ship's, Tiny Naylor's, and Clock's. The design of a Clock coffee shop (*bottom*) near the airport in Westchester featured a triangular sign pylon and triangular windows.

quite nicely into a sprawling tract development or a singular hillside site. The ranch's low profile exuded informality. Its free-flowing, interior living space, which faced a rear terrace or garden through sliding glass doors, provided privacy. Leading the practitioners who experimented with this hybrid was Cliff May, who designed and built an estimated 1,000 variations of the ranch house and leased plans for at least 18,000 more. Countless others were freely adapted, as the style spread across the country and abroad, to stand with the more severe modern house as California's contribution to the look of the 1950s.

This golden age of L.A. architecture also was marked by a wide range of functional, distinctly styled two- and three-story apartment buildings that seemed to pop up almost overnight to meet the pressing need for housing. Not much more than structured stucco boxes, they were decorated with varying stylized, streamline, and futuristic elements to lend them personality. Some also had names scrawled across their often brightly painted facades, such as the Mediterranean, the Caribbean, the Fountain Blu, the Waterworks, and every combination containing the word "villa." Many of the names of the apartment buildings were not unlike the motels they resembled. Reyner Banham described them in his architectural history of L.A. as "dingbats," noting that they represented nearly every style that ever has been through the L.A. meat grinder from, "Tacoburger Aztec to Wavy-line Moderne, from Cape Cod to unsupported Jaoul vaults, from Gourmet Mansardic to Polynesian Gabled and even—in extremity—Modern Architecture." Banham added that as such, the dingbat was "the true symptom of Los Angeles' urban Id trying to cope with the unprecedented appearance of residential densities too high to be subsumed within the illusion of homestead living."

Opposite and below: Wayfarers'
Chapel. Built and landscaped in
1951, this gabeled, glass jewel
box on a bluff in Palos Verdes
was designed by Lloyd Wright
with the expectation that the
Redwod saplings planted around
it would in time embosom the
chapel, which they have.

Actually, most of the apartment buildings
that rose in the postwar years could best be
described as a vernacular modern, in effect,
updated versions of courtyard housing, usually
turned from the street and raised one level to
provide parking for the now essential car. Indeed, some of the decorative elements on the
apartment buildings looked like hood ornaments and grilles taken from cars. While
many of the stucco boxes were quite raw,
others, planned around lushly landscaped
patios featuring swimming pools, could be
quite attractive. Certainly they hinted at the
promise of the L.A. life-style many of the residents were pursuing. Observed John Beach
and John Chase in an insightful essay in *Home
Sweet Home*, "the stucco box provided a living
environment that was a clean, well-lighted
space, at a human scale, for a reasonable price,
and with the popular approval to which high

art modernism aspired, but seldom achieved."

The stucco-box apartment house was just one of a variety of structures rising across L.A., which were characterized by a sort of pluralistic, popular modernism. Supermarkets, furniture stores, clothing shops, gasoline stations, bowling alleys, and car washes, all embraced and exaggerated the structural and material innovations of modernism. Their three-dimensional signs penetrated the sky, while soaring roofs seemed to float in air above walls of glass and brightly lit, plastic-coated interiors. The frugal, Moderne-styled com-mercial structures of the Depression and War years gave way to a futuristic, modern style..

The architecture was born not out of aesthetic concerns but out of marketing. L.A.'s consumers were cruising in cars along commercial strips that seemed to stretch into a suburban infinity. The challenge to store owners and their designers was to catch and tickle the imagination of the passing motorist. And they did just that with a panorama of the future, albeit at curbside. Meanwhile, the downtown retail center was dying, and with it the red- and yellow-car interurban system.

Below: Sleeping Beauty's Castle, the centerpiece of Disneyland, conceived by Walt Disney and opened in 1955.

Another amusement came to L.A. in 1957: the Dodger baseball team, which abandoned Brooklyn to camp out in sunnier, more lucrative Los Angeles. While a new stadium was being built for the franchise in Chavez Ravine a mile north of downtown, the Dodgers played in the Coliseum. The 56,000 - seat Dodger Stadium *(opposite)* eventually opened in 1962.

Taking its place was an expanding freeway system. In a little more than ten years, from the end of the war to 1960, the freeway system in L.A. grew tenfold, to about 250 miles. "More important than the Dodgers or civic buildings in giving Los Angeles its new personality are the ribbons of freeway which are gradually tying the city's scattered pieces together," observed *Life* magazine in the 1950s.

When the Harbor-Pasadena and Hollywood and Santa Ana freeways were connected just north of downtown L.A. in 1953 by a four-level interchange nicknamed "the stack," a photograph of it appeared in dozens of national magazines and on thousands of postcards. "The stack" became the city's most familiar image, just as the Empire State Building represented New York and the Eiffel Tower, Paris. It was a futuristic image, very much in keeping with L.A.'s vision of itself of being the most modern of modern cities. The 1939 World's Fair heralding the future might have

been held in New York, but it was in L.A. in the 1950s that the future was taking shape.

If there was one building type that more than any other brought 1950s modernism to the masses it was embodied in the coffee shops that seemingly dropped from outerspace to rest alongside the highways and byways of L.A. They could beckon or they could repulse, depending on one's mood. Philip Marlowe was not in a good mood one night, in Raymond Chandler's *The Little Sister*, as he cruised from West Hollywood over into the valley, "past the gaudy neons and the false fronts behind them, the sleazy hamburger joints that look like palaces under the colors, the circular drive-ins as gay as circuses with the chipper hard-eyed car hops, the brilliant counters, and the sweaty greasy kitchens that would kill a toad."

Coffee-shop modernism was a flamboyant one, founded on the innovative structural and material tenets of the movement, but expressed in an exaggerated style that for a

The Watts Towers. Said Simon Rodia of his folk art masterpiece after working on it from 1921 to 1954: "I had in mind to do something big, and I did."

time was known as "googie" architecture. The phrase was coined by architecture writer Douglas Haskel when he first saw Googie's restaurant in West Hollywood. Googie's was designed by John Lautner, a former student of Frank Lloyd Wright, who had embraced the new construction technology with a singular, expressive zeal. It was considered by Haskel the epitome of exaggerated, low-brow modernism. The term had a brief vogue in the architectural press and schools, becoming pejorative, a synonym for vulgar design and the corruption of the purity of modernism championed by architects Walter Gropius, Mies van der Rohe, and others.

Nevertheless, "more people came to use and experience modern architecture through the coffee shops in the 1950s than ever visited a building by Gropius," commented architectural historian Alan Hess in his definitive study *Googie*. "Insofar as architecture is a cultural manifestation, the democratization of modern ideas via commercial architecture served an indispensable purpose," added Hess. "The Coffee Shop Modern, however 'corrupted,' fulfilled the one basic idea of Modernism in the way high art projects remaining on the drawing board or built in a single example could not: the structures were actually used and enjoyed by millions."

If there was one place that captured the spirit of L.A. in the 1950s it was thirty miles south of downtown just off the Harbor Boulevard exit of the Santa Ana freeway. There, in 1955, Disneyland opened for business. Behind a giant parking lot and through its turnstiles was nearly every vision of L.A. that had arisen since its founding, albeit pristine, safe, and synthetic. There, beyond a nostalgic, turn-of-

the-century main street, within easy walking distance of one another were adventureland, frontierland, fantasyland, and tomorrowland. But most important, Disneyland was fun, taking advantage of Southern California's benign weather and penchant for make-believe. The park quickly became the region's number-one tourist attraction, reviving in a well-designed and choreographed agglomeration, L.A.'s rich tradition of amusement parks.

But, unlike the earlier parks, which jutted out on pleasure piers festooned with Byzantine-styled bathhouses, roller coasters, and carnival attractions, Disneyland was quite upscale. It was a place of fairy tales come true; where the transportation system of monorails, trains, trams, trolleys, and walking worked; where design was both playful and functional, and where people smiled and, if only for a few hours, shared a sense of community. Walt Disney had turned about seventy-six acres in the city of Anaheim into the epitome of the L.A. mythos.

Just about the time the finishing touches were being applied to Disneyland, a towering, folk-art fretwork of glass and ceramic fragments, seashells, and cement-encrusted structural pipes was being completed in the then nondescript neighborhood in south central L.A. called Watts. Begun in 1921, the so-called Watts Towers were the dream and creation of an immigrant Italian mason named Simon (also Sabbatino, or Sam) Rodia. When he considered the towers finished in 1954, Rodia simply walked away, leaving the city and the world to ponder his creation. Reflecting a generation of hope, innocence, and fantasy, the Watts Towers remain an appropriate symbol of their period's architectural ambience.

8

STUMBLING FORWARD

In spite of all the hopes . . . Los Angeles was becoming neither a Better City nor a City Beautiful nor an Earthly Paradise but a World City, just as complex and cosmopolitan as any conventional city of the past, a city in which almost anything could be found by those who knew where to look for it . . . a city of wild and wonderful and banal buildings, a city of bungalow-slums in junk-strewn gardens, a Mexican city, negro city, Japanese city, a city of oil-wells and art galleries, surfboards and sunsets . . . a failed Jerusalem, a low-density Babylon.

—Mark Girouard, *Cities and People* (1985)

he 1960s began optimistically enough, with the number of jobs and the population to fill them continuing to grow, and standards in architecture and planning rising steadily. L.A. was still on the cutting edge of trends, setting the pace for the country. Architect John Lautner of "googie" fame caused a sensation with a circular house, labeled the Chemosphere, perched on a concrete column jutting out from a steep slope high in the Hollywood hills. Also reaching for the sky, now that the city's 150-foot height limit had been lifted, were plans for a variety of modern, monolithic, office towers. A cluster was planned on a former Westside back lot of 20th Century-Fox Film Studios, renamed Century City, and another was in the works downtown, alongside a monumental cultural complex on Bunker Hill. The hope was that the center, which featured a concert hall and theaters, and its backdrop of glistening office towers, would lift downtown up out of generations of decay to become once again the focal point of the diffuse region.

The Case Study houses were also still generating interest. Though they were getting increasingly expensive, more and more of their adaptations were to be found among the tract housing spreading farther and farther out into the valleys and up the hillsides. In a reaction to the sprawl, the owners of the 144-square-mile Irvine Ranch in Orange County, the country's largest, intact expanse of undeveloped land near an urban setting, decided to do something different. Instead of dividing it up and selling off their holdings to so-called "down-and-dirty," tract developers, they hired L.A. architect William Pereira to devise a master plan to turn the ranch into a futuristic, balanced community of homes, schools,

Left: The Chemosphere. This stylish octagon-shaped house designed by John Lautner descended on L.A. in 1960 like a flying saucer, to perch on a concrete stalk in the Hollywood Hills. Yet the futuristic design was actually quite practical, taking advantage of what had been considered an unbuildable site, leaving the fragile hillside intact and providing a spectacular view of the valley below and the mountains beyond *(below)*.

Previous page opposite: The view downtown from the southwest in 1985. In the foreground, amidst faded commercial and residential buildings, parking lots, and vacant lots, is the gleaming Vista Montoya housing complex, a subsidized condominium project lending new life to the Pico Union neighborhood. It was designed by the firm of Kamnitzer & Cotton.

Century City, master-planned by Welton Beckett and Associates, was begun in the 1960s and is continuing. The corporate International style glistens in a cluster of office towers on the Westside, dominated by two identical, sleek triangular towers designed by Minoru Yamasaki. The cluster was part of a plan drafted by the city that would create satellite centers to relieve pressure on downtown and, not coincidentally, on the freeway system by encouraging office construction in select, scattered sections of the region. The result in Century City was something like a corporate Brasilia.

parks, offices, industry, agricultural and commercial and cultural centers. There were also ambitious plans announced by others for a satellite commercial complex, Warner Center, in the San Fernando Valley, and a planned community, Westlake Village, farther west in the Conejo Valley. Like most ambitious developments in L.A., they were paced by the expanding freeway system.

"We have come to accept with enthusiasm the unprofessional, unappreciative, unskillful butchery of the land that goes under the name of planning," declared Pereira as he began to draft the Irvine plan in the glare of unprecedented national publicity. "Here we have a tremendous opportunity to point people's tastes and expectations in another direction. And we can do it. The sheer size of the place makes almost anything possible." It was a statement very much in keeping with the optimism and dreams expressed a half century before in Dana Bartlett's utopian treatise, *A Better City*.

But the dream of the good life in L.A. soon became haunted by natural disasters, and political and planning disappointments that began in the 1960s and reached into the 1980s. In 1961 a devastating fire destroyed more than 500 homes in Bel Air and Brentwood; in 1963 the Baldwin Hills Dam collapsed, flooding the neighborhood beneath it; in 1971 an earthquake centered in the north San Fernando Valley left sixty-four dead and caused nearly $1 billion in damages; in 1978 fires ravaged Malibu, in 1980 Laurel Canyon, and in 1985 Baldwin Hills. There were also intermittent droughts and floods and landslides. With the concomitant rise in the environmental movement, residents began questioning the pace, siting, and form of development, particularly in the fragile, fire-prone hillsides. But the bulldozing continued, destroying vegetation and vistas, along with visions of a garden city.

The western ridge of downtown took on a decidedly corporate look in the 1970s with the construction of a variety of ultimately bland towers in the International style. A centerpiece of this façade was the cluster of cylindrical towers forming the Bonaventure Hotel, designed by John Portman and Associates, 1975. To the left of the Bonaventure is the twin, 52-story, dark, polished, monolithic towers of Arco plaza, designed by Albert C. Martin and Associates. Farther to the left and also designed by the A. C. Martin firm is the horizontally banded Wells Fargo Building. The towers did lend themselves to some well-composed photographs, especially when viewed from the north and framed by the Alexander Calder sculpture gracing the plaza of the well-executed Security Pacific Bank, another A. C. Martin design. But the scene seemed chilly, even on the warmest summer days.

In 1965 a riot in the predominately low-income, black community of Watts took the lives of thirty-four people. "After 25 years of haphazard growth and unprecedented prosperity, Los Angeles now faces the same tough economic and social problems that confronted older cities years ago," commented *U.S. News & World Report*. Social unrest continued in the form of demonstrations against the lingering war in Southeast Asia. One demonstration touched off a riot in Chicano East L.A. It was in a local hotel after winning the California Democratic presidential primary in 1968 that Robert Kennedy was assassinated. The underside of the L.A. dream was again revealed in the Manson "family" massacres in 1971. In the years following, a grisly succession of serial murders (including the "Hillside Strangler" and the "Night Stalker"), and a general increase in seemingly senseless crime and gang warfare chilled and numbed L.A.

Local government faltered, due in part to an enormously confused and complex regional structure. It consisted of 84 independent municipalities, including the city of Los Angeles, dozens of unincorporated communities, 95 school districts, and 275 special districts, the latter dealing with such services as sanitation, fire protection, and flood control. The result was a lack of a consistent and coordinated policy to deal with pressing planning, environmental, and transportation issues.

The last Red Car of the interurban system ground to a halt on April 8, 1961, completing its final run five minutes late. No one was keeping time when the last trolley stopped running a few years later. Continuing, as they have sporadically since the 1900s, were studies for an alternative mass-transit system, principally a subway, rechristened a metro rail. But the only thing the studies prompted was debate. And as the bureaucrats talked, the city's

Japanese Village Plaza *(below)*, designed by a team headed by David Hyun Associates, was an attempt to aid the Little Tokyo area of downtown, which had been in decline during the 1960s and 1970s. Its entrance marked by a traditional fire tower, the Plaza, lined with one- and two-story shops and restaurants, meanders through the midblock, past a fountain, and under a few Ginkgo trees to create a welcoming pedestrian ambience. As hoped, the Plaza became the centerpiece of the revitalization of the community in the 1980s.

A sympathetic renewal program by the Community Redevelopment Agency revived Spring Street, a downtown strip of substantial but faded palaces of finance. The agency in the 1980s encouraged and aided the recycling of select landmark structures along the street, a National Historic District, and even moved its own offices there. One of the more ambitious and successful projects involved the Security National Bank building, a Classical Revival extravagance designed by John Parkinson in 1916. It was recycled and expanded in 1985 under the direction of the architectural firm of John Sergio Fisher & Associates into a four-theater complex of the Los Angeles Actors Theater (below).

extensive bus system sputtered, and the freeways, though expanding to about seven hundred miles by the mid-1980s, became more and more congested. The result was frustrated drivers and aggravated smog. The state department of transportation (Caltrans) did try in 1976 to "discipline" L.A.'s freeways by encouraging carpooling with the designation of select "diamond lanes" for cars with three or more persons. The action prompted not carpooling, but threats of anarchy, and was abandoned after a few months.

Meanwhile the traffic kept increasing, spilling off the freeways onto local streets, extending rush-hour crushes, and generally causing havoc. City and county agencies responded by widening streets, in the process cutting down trees, narrowing sidewalks, and destroying neighborhood ambience. It was ap-

parent by the mid-1980s that much of L.A. had simply become too dense to work well as a car-oriented city, yet not dense enough and too fragmented for an effective mass-transit system.

The crunch of cars, the smog, and the sprawl, along with the natural and man-made disasters, affected the image of L.A. as lotusland. In the 1960s and 1970s the L.A. dream faded, if not into a nightmare, then into a narrow vision of a city of weirdos on roller skates in pursuit of deep tans and shallow relationships, or hustlers trying to negotiate first liens, second mortgages, and three-movie deals. Coloring the vision was a profusion of fads and fashions, sundry cults, rampant real estate speculation, and shifting fortunes in the aerospace and entertainment industries.

L.A.'s rich architectural history suffered.

The Los Angeles County Museum of Art *(below)* was designed by William Pereira and Associates as a complex of three pavilions in 1964. The museum, designed in a monumental Modern style then popular for such facilities, combined with the Music Center downtown, spurred the cultural emergence of L.A. in the 1960s. A new building and entry *(opposite)* by Hardy Holzman and Pfeiffer linked the disparate elements in 1986. A major piece of the complex is the Robert O. Anderson building fronting Wilshire Boulevard, which completes the quadrant. Its playful, Postmodern, banded façade includes Art Deco and Moderne details that reflect the historic style and tone of the street.

To make way for new projects, dozens of landmarks were demolished. These included stunning houses designed by Greene & Greene, Irving Gill, R. M. Schindler, and Richard Neutra, and a host of commercial delights, such as the Streamline-styled Coulters department store and the spectacular, Art-Deco Richfield office tower. Even the famous Brown Derby, the dateline of so many Hollywood, gossip-column items, was dented and knocked off its block. Also being pummeled were long-established neighborhoods famous for their period architecture. These included, among others, the North University Park, Alverado Terrace, and West Adams areas, with their Victorian, Shingle, and Craftsman-styled houses, and Lafayette Square and Country Club Estates with their neo-Classic and Moorish mansions.

The decay and destruction of the landmarks prodded the region's long-dormant preservationist movement into action. Banding together to form new, more powerful and determined groups, such as the Los Angeles Conservancy and Hollywood Heritage and Pasadena Heritage, the preservationists strove mightily to raise the collective public consciousness, and to protect and encourage the recycling of landmarks. Successes included the Art-Deco-adorned Wiltern Theater, the Gartz

Court bungalow complex, the stately Biltmore and Hollywood Roosevelt hotels, the moderne Pan Pacific Auditorium, and a score of downtown, neo-Classical office buildings. They also worked to stabilize older residential neighborhoods and commercial districts, prodding city agencies to expand their landmark designation efforts and to establish rehabilitation and restoration programs. The battle to save architectural landmarks had been joined, and with it efforts began to preserve L.A.'s paradoxical essence and ambience that were being lost in the region's inexorable growth.

Beyond the disasters and the distortions, L.A. was maturing as a city, enjoying a blossoming cultural life. Due in part to the efforts of heiress Caroline Ahmanson, a County Museum of Art opened in 1964, designed by William Pereira. Personal fortunes also created, in the 1970s, the Norton Simon and J. Paul Getty museums and expanded the Huntington. And in the 1980s, an imaginative city redevelopment agency spurred the construction of two museums of contemporary art downtown, one a sparkling Postmodernist gem designed by Arata Isozaki, and the other a striking recycling of a municipal garage by Frank Gehry. The County Museum and the Getty both expanded, the latter onto a sprawling site in the hills above Sunset Boulevard in Brentwood forming a cultural complex, designed by Richard Meier, which is scheduled to be completed in the early 1990s.

What Ahmanson had done for art, Dorothy Chandler did for music, generating support for a music center crowning Bunker Hill.

The colonnaded neo-Classical center designed by Welton Becket opened in 1969 to provide a home for a world-renowned orchestra and a major drama group. Other music and theater groups flowered, fed by the diverse talents attracted by the entertainment industry. As art galleries and artist communities were stimulated by the new and expanding museums, there at last seemed to be "culture" in L.A.

Local colleges and universities grew, in population, and in prestige as centers of research and athletic training. The nationally successful teams of USC and UCLA whetted L.A.'s appetite for sports, attracting to the region the baseball Dodgers and Angels, the football Rams and Raiders and the basketball Lakers and Clippers. The profusion of teams and championships generated for L.A. a wellspring of civic pride that, in part, resulted in the city's exuberant success hosting the 1984 Olympics.

Colleges and universities contributed to the development of a variety of high-tech and health-care industries. Their success also fed the city's expanding role as a financial center for the Pacific rim, taking the title away from San Francisco. And, as trade increased with Japan and other Asian countries in the 1970s and 1980s L.A.'s role as a corporate and commercial power became second only to New York City.

Unfortunately L.A.'s skyline did not reflect her new role as a center of commerce and finance. The first office towers (nicknamed smogscrapers) to rise downtown, after the height limit had been lifted, were mostly monolithic, glass-box structures. Though varying in detailing and coloring, they were, with a few exceptions, generally bland. And the few that were not bland, such as the soaring glass cylinders of the Bonaventure Hotel designed by John Portman, the well-detailed, twin Arco

While the exterior of the Crystal Cathedral, wrapped in a mirrored glass skin, is elegant, the interior, when the light is right, is stunning. With its glass roof and walls braced by space trusses in the form of a web of white pipes, the interior glistens on sunny days and glows on others.

towers by Albert C. Martin, and the rich-bricked Broadway Plaza by Charles Luckman, were badly sited.

Marvelous opportunities were lost for more distinguished developments. One was the so-called Grand Avenue proposal of builder Robert Maguire, orchestrated by planner Harvey Perloff heading a team of diverse designers that included Frank Gehry, Hardy Holzman Pfeiffer Associates, Lawrence Halprin, Robert Kennard, Ricardo Legoretta, Barton Meyers, Charles Moore, and Cesar Pelli. Responding to a competition sponsored by the city's Community Redevelopment Agency in 1979 to develop eleven prime acres on Bunker Hill, the team's scheme was a rich variegated version of New York's Rockefeller Center. Instead of being monumental, the scheme was playful and included a variety of public spaces to encourage the pedestrian life L.A. was sadly missing. Though the scheme won broad critical approval, it was rejected by the city agency in favor of a safe, slick reworking of a typical urban renewal solution labeled California Plaza and submitted by a team headed by architect Arthur Erickson.

The playful Grand Avenue proposal was ahead of its time, for a few years later, in the early 1980s, corporations wanting to enhance their image, together with tenants in search of prestige addresses, began to seek out such distinctive designs. Sensitive to their market, developers responded by encouraging architects to produce more expressive late-Modern and Postmodern designs. Among the more successful of the new structures that followed were the smooth, red granite, polygonal-towered complex of Crocker Center, designed by the firm of Skidmore, Owings and Merrill and completed in 1985; a spirited, colorful festival market by the Jerde Partnership at the foot of the Citicorp complex in 1986; and a Post-

modern concoction on Wilshire Boulevard by Kohn, Pedersen and Fox completed in 1987. Also on the boards was a delicately detailed, seventy-three-story tower by I.M. Pei & Partners. By 1987 the towers downtown were forming a critical mass necessary to lend visual drama and a focus to the L.A. skyline.

Beyond downtown, office towers of indifferent quality began to sprout in the 1970s in select satellite centers that had been loosely planned to focus growth. The centers included, among others, Century City, Warner Center, Westwood, and downtown Burbank, Glendale, Pasadena, Santa Monica, Long Beach, Costa Mesa, Santa Ana, and Newport Beach. However, office towers also rose like swollen, awkward thumbs seemingly at random in such areas as Brentwood, West L.A., and Sherman Oaks, much to the chagrin of adjoining residential neighborhoods. Taking advantage of loopholes in the zoning code, the towers blocked views, flooded streets with traffic, and rudely informed surrounding residents that L.A. was becoming more urban and more chaotic.

Adding to the chaos was the development of a variety of mammoth shopping malls. While some malls, such as Fox Hills Mall, designed by Cesar Pelli and Victor Gruen, worked well as regional centers with easy access to freeways, others, plopped down in established neighborhoods, did much damage to the immediate area and to the older shopping districts from which they took customers. If the design of the hulking, brown-gray Beverly Center at Beverly and La Cienega boulevards was not bad enough, its construction in 1982 weakened the frail economics of the stores in the nearby historic, Art-Deco district of Wilshire Boulevard. And though the design by the Jerde Partnership of the Westside Pavilion in Rancho Park was an engaging Post-

Below: The Tillman Water Reclamation Plant, designed by Anthony Lumsden of the firm of Daniel, Mann, Johnson & Mendenhall, and completed in 1984. Lumsden took the San Fernando Valley municipal facility with an unappealing function and made it into an attractive, expressive, glistening high-tech complex.

Lumsden could almost always be counted on to apply an inventive spirit to a particular style. A decade earlier, in 1973, he broke away from the bland, boxy International style to encase a Beverly Hills office building in an undulating, black glass curtain wall.

One of the more challenging architectural problems in L.A. in the 1980s was to reconstruct and expand the Los Angeles International Airport to handle the enormous increase of airplanes, automobiles, and people passing through it. While the airport continued to operate, a roadway was doubledecked, parking increased, traffic rerouted, and new terminals constructed. The largest and most successful, in both function and form, was the international terminal, designed by a team of architects, engineers, and landscape architects headed by the firm of Dworsky Associates.

modernist pastiche, its siting in 1985 also damaged the surrounding area. Where the malls could not fit, mini-malls were built, usually at a busy intersection in a neighborhood shopping district, destroying street scapes and discouraging pedestrian life. As for planning in the city, it became an afterthought.

Planning also suffered across the region, where it often was diluted in a flood of political, environmental, and economic concerns. In Irvine, growth was directed as had been generally outlined in the 1960s master plan by Pereira. But the tone was very stratified and squeaky clean, and the style bland. The planning also was auto-oriented, the community life focused on recreation, and the design of much of the housing traditional adaptations of Spanish and American colonial styles, sprinkled with a little English Tudor and French Chateau. That is what the buyers wanted, and that is what they got from Irvine, as well as from Westlake, and in lesser degrees and varying styles from other sprouting subdivisions.

Among the more interesting larger efforts in the modern idiom was the sleek Xerox

The Torie Steel boutiques on Rodeo Drive *(below left)* were a welcome departure from the avaricious development of shopping strips and mini malls that were marring the city's streetscapes in the 1980s. Designed with sensitivity by Johannes Van Tilburg & Partners, the five-shop complex of joined and related spaces presented a well-scaled and intimate façade of individual stores to the fashionable Beverly Hills street. The rusticated details were said by Van Tilburg to have been inspired by shops found on the Via Dela Spiga in Milan.

Another project that responds to its environment, adding verve to Pico Boulevard in Santa Monica, was this design *(below right)* of an architect's office by Ross/Wou International. A classical motif, the arch, was applied to a flat storefront and also became the organizing principle in the interior, where it was used in a series of planes set at 45° angles. The arched silhouettes lead to the raised conference room, whose curved and vividly colored façade animated the busy office.

building in El Segundo and the severe Art Center College of Design in Pasadena by Craig Ellwood. The idiom was reorganized by Cesar Pelli and Anthony Lumsden, then of the firm of DMJM, in their 1967 design of the Teledyne Laboratories in Northridge. Pelli went on as a member of Gruen Associates to design in a neo-Modern style in 1975 the strikingly elegant, cobalt-blue, glass Pacific Design Center in West Hollywood. His addition to the center planned for 1989 also promises to be distinctive. Lumsden stayed with DMJM and designed in 1973 an undulating, glass-skinned Manufacturers Bank building in Beverly Hills, and in 1984 a high-tech extravaganza of a wastewater treatment plant in the San Fernando Valley. Also remarkable were a sensitively scaled, exotic Japanese Village Plaza by David Hyun in 1979; a shimmering Crystal Cathedral in Garden Grove by Philip Johnson and John Burgee in 1980; an expressive, sleek transportation center in Santa Monica by Kappe, Lotery and Boccato in 1984; a well-detailed County Government Center in San Bernardino by Kurt Meyer in 1985; and the exquisitely sculpted L.A. Museum of Contem-

porary Art by Arata Isozaki in 1986. Each in their respective styles carried forward L.A.'s tradition of innovative design.

The residential designs of Ray Kappe, A. Quincy Jones, Helmut Schulitz, John Blanton, Charles Moore, John Mutlow, Rebecca Binder, Ron Goldman, Randy Washington, and the firms of Kamnitizer and Cotton; Moore, Ruble, Yudell; and Solberg and Lowe attempted, with varying skill and success, to adapt modern technology, cloaked in a regional style, to a wide range of challenging sites and budgets.

More controversial was a loosely formed community of designers centered in Venice experimenting under the banner of architecture as art. Most prominent among the designers was Frank Gehry, who in the mid-1970s broke out of the cube of modernism to explore a form of architectural minimalism. The efforts of Gehry and Thom Mayne, Michael Rotondi, Eric Owen Moss, and Craig Hodgetts, among the more prominent, were scattered individualistic designs of strained geometry and perverted materials. Some worked

as "art"; some did not. While not of particular importance locally, the funky and punk designs did attract international attention, fulfilling an often parochial, preconceived view among visiting critics and peers of a spaced-out, L.A. architecture scene.

"For a while now, Los Angeles has been producing an embarrassingly rich little pocket of naughty new buildings that must be seen as more than the mere exuberance of an irrelevant Tinseltown," declared British architect Peter Cook in a June 1984 issue of *Progressive Architecture* magazine. The issue featured as its cover story a fragmented structure pasted together with fiberglass shingles, galvanized sheet metal, plywood veneer, ceramic tile, concrete block, and stucco. The self-advertisement concocted by Moss was heralded with a snicker as "the quintessential L.A. freeway house." The L.A. design community, which just a few years before had been known for its pursuit of architecture as a social art, winced.

Meanwhile, L.A. was becoming increasingly international. The most American

Stirring up the architectural scene in L.A. since the mid-1970s has been Frank Gehry, experimenting with materials and forms in attempts to say something about art as architecture, or architecture as art, or simply to have his buildings establish a vague dialogue with themselves, their context, and the design and construction process. Whatever, they have attracted healthy attention, as well as mixed critical reviews. Quite successful is Gehry's design for the Loyola Law School *(below)* in the Pico Union neighborhood southwest of downtown. The structure at the center with its columns of galvanized steel hints at a raw Classicism, while the campus with its free-standing columns suggests a Roman forum. Gehry said he purposely "unorganized"

the campus so it would look "un-designed." But the forms seem quite conscious of historical styles, playfully applied. The total is a witty, modest, intown campus of fragmented structures that enliven the school and the surrounding neighborhoods. In contrast, the jumble of the Aerospace Building *(below)*, which Gehry designed for the California Museum of Science and Industry in Exposition Park, does not function particularly well. But it is provocative.

of cities, in 1985 L.A. had more residents of Mexican descent than any other city other than Mexico City, more Koreans than any city outside Korea, and the largest Japanese, Armenian, Iranian, Filipino, Vietnamese, Thai, and British communities in the United States. Whether it was the movies and TV shows depicting L.A. as a sort of new-world nirvana, or what, it was to L.A. they came, making the city the most popular port of entry in the United States, legally and illegally. The heaviest inflow have been Hispanics, principally from Mexico and Central America, followed by Asians filtering in from Korea, Japan, China, Cambodia, Malaysia, Sri Lanka, and Samoa. The melting pot that had been L.A. became in the 1980s a sort of gazpacho, with a side order of Asian-Pacific stew.

Also becoming sort of a stew, albeit of styles, was L.A.'s architecture. Always idiosyncratic, the architecture seemed more than ever to reflect the tenor of the confused and conflicted times, and their diverse and sometimes divisive trends. It ranged from very controlled and, generally, weak copies of the severe, modern idiom of the International style to intuitive, often pretentious, designs under the broad classification of Postmodernism. There were also provocative experiments with expressive high-tech materials, studied neo-Modern and late-Modern efforts, strained attempts to be different, imaginative restorations and recyclings of historic structures, and a broad range of practical, programmatic structures. But no style dominated. It was a time of eclecticism—the fashioning of singular objects on singular city and suburban landscapes. Somehow the mix seemed appropriate to an egalitarian L.A.

In the design of his own house (*below*) in 1968 in Rustic Canyon, Ray Kappe extended the clean lines of modernism, clad them in redwood, opened up the interior, and let the landscaping over- whelm the exterior. The result was a Craftsman Modern. Kappe's design of the nearby Sultan House in 1976 (*bottom*) was even more expansive.

Residential design in L.A. was jolted in 1978 by the Gehry House *(below)*. In expanding what had been a nondescript Santa Monica structure, Gehry tested a deconstructivist theory. He exposed behind glass the wood framing of the original house and in building the expansion used bits and pieces of corrugated sheet metal, chain link fencing, and raw plywood and studs, and generally played games with forms and perspectives. More typical in meeting the more common challenges of residential construction was the Mitchell House in Malibu *(bottom)*, designed by Ron Goldman. The challenges included a small, narrow site and the desire for both privacy and distinctive design. Goldman's design was reasonable and sensitive.

The L.A. style? Ever idiosyncratic, it has ranged from monumental Modern, to anti-Modern, to Postmodern. The design by Welton Beckett and Associates of the Music Center *(opposite top)* in the mid-1960s mixed monumentalism with moxie to come up with a downtown complex that can host a variety of events, from the Academy Awards to opera, musicals, and experimental dramas. The Temporary Contemporary *(bottom)* in Little Tokyo was to be temporary, while the new Museum of Contemporary Art was being built. But the anti-Modern renovation of a deteriorated municipal garage in 1983 by Frank Gehry was so successful that the museum was made permanent. Meanwhile, the new museum *(below and opposite bottom)*, designed in a singular Modern style by Arata Isozaki, was opened in 1986, a well-chiseled gem in the crown of Bunker Hill.

184

Downtown skyline, 1986.

The L.A. style, continued. The soaring, smooth, red-granite-clad angled towers of Crocker Center (*left*), designed by the firm of Skidmore, Owings and Merrill, when completed in 1985 was a distinguished addition to the corporate façade of downtown. But the well-detailed building could be in any city. Much more individualistic is the Pacific Design

Center (*below*), designed by Cesar Pelli and Gruen Associates and built in 1975. The hulking, reflective cobalt-blue glass building has become a focal point for West Hollywood and its interior design community. The 1984 Summer Olympics lent a distinct style to L.A. in the imaginative use of temporary structures, graphics, and color, orchestrated by the Jerde Partnership and the design firm of Sussman/Prejza. *Below right:* A tower that had marked the west entry to Exposition Park and the Coliseum. After the Olympic Games, the festive pastel palette was applied to a populist Postmodern-styled Westside Pavilion shopping mall, (*opposite bottom*). The Olympics were gone, but the look remained. The relaxed life-style of L.A. and a respect for the surrounding landscape and architectural tradition were combined in the design of St. Matthew's Episcopal Church in the Pacific Palisades (*bottom*). It was designed in 1982 by the firms of Moore Ruble Yudell, architects, and Campbell and Campbell, landscape architects.

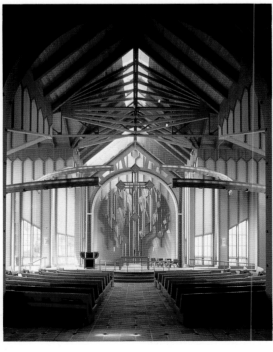

9

LOST AND FOUND

All those hundreds of [Cliff] May ranch houses, big and small, like all the hundreds of thousands of anonymous dwellings that make up the loosely woven fabric of the city, are embodiments of dreams that, against all odds, have managed to come true. Wracked by floods, droughts, and earthquakes, in terms of safety Los Angeles might just as well be perched on the shimmering upper slopes of Vesuvius, but it doesn't matter: nothing is as outrageous as a dream, and a city founded on dreams and scorning prudence is likely to endure forever.
    —Brendan Gill, *The Dream Come True: Great Houses of Los Angeles* (1980)

The fires that periodically ravage L. A.'s fragile hillsides can be frightening. Flames are carried on savage Santa Ana winds, which race from canyon to canyon, igniting the tinder-dry chaparral and eucalyptus trees in violent explosions, and leaving a wake of scorched earth covered with a thick, powdery blanket of ash. But within months after the fires and the rains that usually follow, plant shoots begin to sprout from the blackened limbs of the trees and out of the ground, as the hillsides quietly heal themselves. And within a few years, in another example of the region's regenerative powers, the hillsides are again in brilliant bloom.

While the region's vegetation is amazingly resilient, the landscape, when in the grasping hands of man, is not. Once bulldozed to make way for roads and houses, it is permanently altered. And when the bulldozing levels hills, destroys vistas, and disrupts the ecology, and the resulting housing clashes in color and context with the landscape, lost is the natural beauty of L.A.'s spectacular setting.

Once a residential retreat, recreational resource, and verdant backdrop for the city, the mountains that form L.A.'s tiara have suffered. The losses have been particularly acute over the last few decades as developers search and scratch for new building sites, turning once idyllic, verdant hillside and canyon communities into sloping, suburban sprawls, the houses on raw earth pads shouldering one another for a view.

But the losses have also made residents and environmentalists more aware of the beauty they once found in the singular natural setting of L.A. They have formed fledgling associations to lobby for more protection and

Lost and found: Being edged off the Civic Center site where it had stood for a half century is the L.A. County Hall of Records (*below left*). Upon completion of the Criminal Courts Building on the same site in the early 1960s, the Hall of Records was demolished. More fortunate was the Pellissier Building (*below right*) with its Zigzag Moderne-styled tower and its ornate, ornamented Wiltern Theater. Designed in 1930 by Morgan, Walls & Clements, with G. A. Lansburgh shaping the theater and Anthony Heinsbergen the murals, the complex was to be demolished in 1979. It was saved by the real estate development firm of Ratkovich & Bowers and restored in 1985.

Lost: The Richfield Building (*opposite*) downtown, an Art Deco masterpiece designed in 1928 by Morgan, Walls & Clements. It was replaced in 1972 by the twin gray granite-sheathed Arco Towers.

Previous page opposite: The view west of the tiled, pyramid-topped tower of the Central Library, with one of the twin Arco towers the backdrop.

Found: A modest Mediterranean Revival building (*opposite*) on West Seventh Street, downtown. Designed by Morgan & Walls in 1922 as a jewelry store and threatened with demolition in the 1970s, it was saved by Clifton's and restored as a restaurant.

Found: The Farmers and Merchants Bank (*below*), still standing and operating as a bank in all its Beaux Arts glory at Fourth Street and Main. It had been designed in the early 1900s by Dodd and Richards. Also persevering as

part of the Olvera Street and El Pueblo de Los Angeles State Historical Park downtown is the Mercedes Theater (*bottom*). The Italianate design is attributed to Ezra Keysor and dates from 1869.

now keep watch over the hillsides, wary of developers and compliant city administrations. While some of the associations are more parochial than others, they do reflect a new-found spirit in L.A., embodying a healthy respect for the region's fragile landscape and ambience.

Just as the hillside residents have rallied to the defense of their city, so have residents of the communities in the basins, valleys, and beaches. They, too, have recognized that lost in the city's frenzied growth were just those elements that had attracted them to L.A. and to particular communities. The losses have been grievous.

In many communities, the city's rich architectural heritage of distinctive, well-scaled and well-crafted homes and courts in sensitively planned and landscaped neighborhoods have been demolished, often to make way for speculative, overscaled, pretentious houses or dingbat apartment projects. Among the landmark residential structures destroyed have been Greene and Greene's Libby House in Pasadena, Gill's Dodge House in Hollywood, Schindler's Lowes House in Eagle Rock, and Neutra's Von Sternberg House in Northridge, stunning structures that had in their time established L.A. as a city of innovative architectural delights. Lost.

Meanwhile, in the beach towns, ocean-front properties have been overbuilt; access to the beaches made difficult; and the once pure water and sparkling sand sullied. In other communities, commercial complexes have been allowed to encroach into residential areas, their office towers casting shadows over backyards and their daily rush-hour traffic clogging local streets. Badly hurt by the seemingly random development of shopping malls and mini-malls are the established retail districts in the Wilshire and Beverly-Fairfax

Found: The Gamble House (*below*), by Charles and Henry Greene, survives because of the generosity of the Gamble family, the foresight of the University of Southern California, the concern of the Friends and Docent Council of the Gamble House, and the pride of the city of Pasadena. One of Frank Lloyd Wright's more graceful experiments with pre-cast ornamental concrete block structures, the Freeman House (*bottom*) survives because of a private owner who cares.

Found: L.A.'s variety of singular architectural styles. Over the years the styles have included a range of Victorian (*top*), such as the houses crowning Angelino Heights that were erected in the 1880s and that still survive. Spanish Revival, the preferred style in the 1920s, evoking in various fanciful forms the myth of the city's Hispanic traditions, is still quite popular. Typical of this style are the duplex apartments (*center*) in the Carthay Circle area. A more recent vogue has been High Tech, such as the Santa Monica condominium (*bottom*), designed with a flair by Rebecca Binder and Jim Stafford.

areas, among others, and those along Ventura, Colorado, and Whittier boulevards. Other retail areas, such as Westwood Village and Main Street in Santa Monica, have suffered from success and have lost long-term busi-nesses to short-term trendy shops. A commer-cial architecture has appeared that in its attempt to achieve a distinct identity rends the brittle city fabric with isolated structures that are out of scale and context. These include, among many, a Postmodernist shopping mall in West Hollywood, and out-of-character office towers in West Los Angeles.

Less dramatic but no less insidious, in nibbling away at the essence of L.A., have been a variety of mindless, street-widening projects, which have destroyed trees, landscap-ing, and lawns, and narrowed sidewalks just so a left-hand turn lane can be created to accommodate traffic. The city's frail pedestrian ambience has been damaged by the street widenings, and by the lost opportunities to make sidewalks more attractive with plantings and places to sit.

Even residents wedded to their cars are beginning to ask whether there is more to liv-ing in L.A. than just being able to drive to and from work, shopping, and the beaches. They question whether their neighborhoods should not be more than back-lot facades, mounted along boulevards that serve as decorated sound walls; whether their shopping districts should not be more than anonymous malls in a sea of parking.

The need to move cars and park them is slowly suffocating downtown and the other commercial centers of the region. But whether this will prompt more people to consider car-pooling, or to take a bus, seems unlikely in a society that loves its cars. Persisting as a hope-ful alternative is a metro rail, but it has been hampered by poor planning and the lack of a

Found: 818 Seventh Street (*right*). Designed in 1925 by Curlett and Bellman as a furniture store in an Italian Renaissance Revival style, it was renovated in 1986 as an office building. Its entrance was said to have been inspired by the Strozzi Palace in Florence. The Fine Arts Building at 811 Seventh Street (*below*) was designed in 1927 by Walter & Eisen in a Spanish Renaissance Revival style. It was renovated by Ratkovich & Bowers in 1983.

Lost and found: The Brown Derby restaurant opened in 1926 on Wilshire Boulevard to become a favorite haunt of Hollywood celebrities for nearly a half century. It was dented badly in an aborted demolition in the early 1980s, was then cleaned and blocked, but unfortunately in 1986 was put on the back of a roof of a two-story development.

needed, long-range financial commitment from the federal government to build it. Meanwhile, there is a grave irony to the realization that the freedom to drive and park at ease has been lost in L.A.'s inexorable growth—a growth that had been spurred by that freedom.

From the Covinas in the east to Playa del Rey in the west, and from Newport in the south to Pasadena in the north, residents are quick to point out that the growth is similar to what they thought they had escaped when they moved from New York, Chicago, Hong Kong, Seoul, and Mexico City. That the growth is what created the opportunities that attracted them to L.A., and to which they have also contributed, is recognized at best with a nod. Like L.A. itself, Angelenos are full of contradictions.

What they do recognize with increasing passion is that the better life L.A. had pro-

mised has been lost somewhere along the denuded streets with their narrow, uninviting sidewalks, beneath the polluted water off select beaches, in the fumes from the clogged traffic, in the shadows of monolithic office towers, and on the subbasement floor of a stygian parking structure. But with the same optimism that brought them and previous generations to L.A., Angelenos know that the promise still exists. In the land of the perpetual spring, hope springs eternal.

This hope for a better life, or simply to protect what now tenuously exists, has in recent years fomented community action to block street widenings, to halt the whittling away of parklands, to stop the destruction of landmarks, and end the construction of a variety of voracious, commercial and residential projects. Citizen groups have also prompted redesigns and modifications of projects to make them more acceptable, such as reducing

Lost: The Dodge House (*below*), built in 1916 in West Hollywood and considered one of Irving Gill's most accomplished designs. It was auctioned off by the Los Angeles Board of Education in the mid-1970s to the highest bidder, who had it demolished to make way for an apartment development.

heights, requiring more landscaping, relocating garage entrances, and softening colors. Their actions, in turn, have led to tougher zoning codes, and a reexamination and fine-tuning of community plans. Although the groups are often in opposition to public and private proposals, and government is usually reactive, both stumble forward, groping for their lost L.A. in the dust of debates over development.

Well-designed, sensitive projects have succeeded, such as Crocker Center downtown, the Japanese Village in Little Tokyo, Crestwood Hills in Brentwood, condo complexes in the Pico Union neighborhood and in Santa Monica, an outdoor cafe in West Los Angeles. But most have been created by imaginative private citizens and inspired public servants, not because of the city's planning practices, but often in spite of them. When it comes to ur-

banity, L.A. takes what it can get in the grab bag of growth.

While residents know what they have lost, they are not exactly sure what they expect to find in their concerted, often conscientious, sometimes contentious, actions to participate in the shaping of their communities. But the residents do recognize, however reluctantly, that they cannot turn back the clock; the one constant in the city is change, just as it has been since its settlement in 1781.

The fact is that L.A. is no longer a low-density, landscaped city, or a garden city of small-scale neighborhoods and single-family houses, or a city of private spaces, backyards, and enclosed patios, rather than public spaces. It still has those attributes, but in fewer and smaller pockets. What L.A. *is* becoming is more urban. It is more of a city in the traditional sense, with crowded sidewalks, intensely

Lost: Coulters Department Store was designed in a slick Streamline Moderne style by Stiles Clements in 1938 to grace the so-called Miracle Mile in the Wilshire district. It was unceremoniously demolished in 1980.

204

Lost: The Streamline Moderne apartment complex on Wilshire Boulevard near Beverly Glen was designed by Milton Black in 1940. It was demolished in the late 1970s to make way for an apartment tower.

Lost: Tiny Naylor's, a landmark of the 1950s and one of the last drive-ins in the L.A. basin, was demolished in 1984.

Lost: The Carthay Circle Theater *(opposite)*, designed in a rich Spanish Baroque style by Dwight Gibbs, opened in 1926 with the world premiere of Cecil B. De Mille's *The Volga Boatman.* It also was the site in 1939 of the Hollywood premiere of *Gone With the Wind.* The film returned to the theater in 1968 and played there for almost a year. At the end of the run in 1969 the theater was demolished for an office complex.

Lost: The Goodyear Tire plant in South Central L.A., an imposing industrial complex built in 1922 in a modified Romanesque style with a touch of Italianate unusual for such structures. It was demolished in the early 1980s.

Lost: The Trinity Methodist Church downtown *(below)*, designed in 1903 in a Romanesque Revival style by Theodore Eisen, was demolished one weekend in 1982. It was followed in 1983 by the First United Methodist Church *(bottom left)*. The prominent downtown church had been designed by John C. Austin in a Spanish Renaissance Revival style and built with authority in 1921. Its site was made into a parking lot for the gas company, to await future office expansion. An earlier downtown victim to the march of commerce was the brick Byzantine-styled, turn-of-the-century B'nai B'rith synagogue *(bottom right)*.

209

used parks and playgrounds, dense housing developments, distinct ethnic districts, and increased cultural attractions.

The transformation from a garden city into something new, certainly different, is being spurred in part by the waves of immigrants and migrants more accustomed to the bustle, and limitations, of cities. The single-family house with a private yard may still be the L.A. ideal, but, with escalating land and housing costs and increased densities, it is no longer relatively easy to obtain. More available, and more common, are town houses and apartments, both condominium and rental. The result is less private space, and a more urban L.A.

Yet L.A. is far from being in the mold of traditional world cities, with their towering skylines, dominant downtown districts, and mass-transit systems tying the surrounding metropolitan areas together in well-defined, established knots of commercial, political, social, and economic stratification. No image dominates; no skyline like New York City; no boulevards as in Paris; no churches as in Rome; no Boston Common; no White House; no cable cars. And no monotony, not with the city's encyclopedia of architectural styles.

Somehow appearing quite appropriate, across the L.A. cityscape, are adobes, log cabins, Spanish haciendas, prairie bungalows, ranch houses, a Hansel-and-Gretel hut, French chateaux, and English country estates, as well as starkly modern and high-tech homes. In L.A., a man's house may be his castle, and a castle his house. There are also buildings shaped like ships, a hot-dog stand like a hot dog, a photo shop like a camera, movie theaters like temples, and hotels like spaceships—programmatic and vernacular architecture designed to catch one's eye. But few are pretentious or precious, designed as they

Found: The wedding-cake top of the Pasadena City Hall (*opposite*), designed by John Bakewell, Jr., and Arthur Brown, Jr., 1927.

Found: The Beaux Arts dome of the Pantages Theater downtown (*below*), a 1911 concoction by Morgan & Walls.

Found: A ramped, sharply angled shopping court topped by a futuristic spire on Rodeo Drive in Beverly Hills. Designed by Frank Lloyd Wright in 1953.

213

are with a touch of guile and leavened with an engaging humor.

There has been more distinguished work, too. "In architecture, and the other arts that stand upon the immediate availability of technical aids, the ill-defined city of the Angels has a well-defined place of honour," declared architectural historian Reyner Banham in his 1971 study of Los Angeles. "Any city that could produce in just over half a century the Gamble House, Disneyland, the Dodge House, the Watts Towers, the Lovell houses, no fewer than 23 buildings by the Lloyd Wright clan, the freeway system, the arcades of Venice, power stations like Huntington Beach, the Eames House, the Universal City movielots, the Schindler House . . . such a city is not one on which anybody who cares about architecture can afford to turn his back and walk away without a word further. Such a very large body of first-class and highly original architecture cannot be brushed off as an accident, an irrelevance upon the face of an indifferent dystopia."

Beyond architecture there are the communities, many of which still reflect the small-town and village qualities of friendly neighbors and solicitous merchants; communities that engender a pride and identity among residents, as well as a protective feeling for a par-

Found: The Powers House (*opposite*), designed in the early 1900s by Arthur L. Haley in a romantic Mission Revival style for Pomeroy Powers as the centerpiece for his Alvarado Terrace subdivision south of downtown. The Powers House and other grand styles of the day survive on the north side of the terrace. The Wrigley mansion (*top*), designed by G. Lawrence Stimson as a classical revival-inspired mansion for the chewing gum king in 1911, set the style for South Orange Grove Boulevard in Pasadena. It survives as the headquarters of the Tournament of Roses Association. Scattered across L.A., and surviving because they are loved and cherished, are a variety of eclectic bungalows and, more rare, stone houses, built in the early 1900s. The bungalow (*center*) and the stone house (*bottom*) face each other at the intersection of Olive and Ninth streets in Burbank.

Found: El Alisal (*the Sycamores*) was the creation of maverick writer and editor Charles Fletcher Lummis. He built the house himself in Highland Park over a fifteen-year period, using stones from the nearby Arroyo Seco, hand-hewn timbers, and his romantic image of Southern California. The singular Craftsman Mission-styled structure was completed in 1910.

Found: The Van Rossem House (*below*) in Pasadena began as a Craftsman cottage designed by Charles and Henry Greene in 1903. They remodeled it a few years later for a new owner, adding, among other things, the timbered front porch. Built in 1910, the comfortable Gartz Court complex of bungalows was slated for demolition in 1983 to make way for a condo development. But the city of Pasadena joined with the local preservation society to save the bungalows, move them one by one to a new site, and restore and remodel them (*bottom*).

218

ticular way of life. These qualities appear to be increasing as the city pushes in on the frayed edges of the varied communities. L.A. is not just Hollywood, or "Hollyweird" as some locals call it, but rather Hollywood is just one distinct, disparate community among many.

Certainly, parts of L.A., such as the Pacific Palisades or Mt. Washington, can be as provincial as a New England hamlet; Westwood as exuberantly youthful as Berkeley; Hancock Park as private as New York's Park Avenue; Carthay Circle as proud of its architecture as Charlestown, South Carolina; Venice as eccentric as Key West; Boyle Heights as boisterous as parts of Mexico City; and West Hollywood as spirited as London's Chelsea. Even downtown, with its new office complexes, landmark districts, and expanding cultural attractions and housing, combined with the lively ethnic communities of Chinatown and Little Tokyo, is beginning to have a look and feel worthy of a metropolis. The resulting mix in many ways resembles London, a city also of urban and suburban villages. Though L.A. certainly does not have the traditions of London, neither has it the pretensions.

L.A. may have lost its youth, in its growth from a cowtown to a boomtown; its exoticism, as it swelled into a suburban sprawl; its innocence, as it sprouted into a world city. It may indeed be a failed Jerusalem, or a Babylon, its arcadian dream tarnished from years of insensitive development, the destruction of landmarks, and smog. Yet L.A. continues to be unique, a marvelous mix of cultures and design, prideful and compelling, a fractured glimpse of the future—now.

UNION RESCUE MISSI
— 226 SO. Main St. —

ACKNOWLEDGMENTS

220

Many individuals contributed to this book, providing assistance, insight, and encouragement. At the risk of offending some whom I do not mention, I want to thank my editor at Crown Publishers, Barbara Grossman, for suggesting the book and for her enthusiasm; my editors at the *Los Angeles Times*, in particular Jean Sharley Taylor, Robert Epstein, and Dick Turpin, for giving me the opportunity to explore at will the L.A. landscape; and both Ruthann Lehrer of the Los Angeles Conservancy and Claire Bogaard of Pasadena Heritage, for exciting my interest in the region's rich architectural history.

Deserving special thanks also are Julius Shulman, who contributed, in addition to his marvelous photography, a valued historical perspective; Dana Levy and Tish O'Connor of Perpetua Press, who with kind humor and valued friendship took the jumble of words and images and made them whole; Marilyn Kelker, who, while I was in the final throes of writing, brought a semblance of order to my professional life; and countless others whom I met in my wandering across the region and who shared with me their knowledge, joy, frustrations, and disappointments about L.A. More than any landmark, setting, or view, it was the people I frankly enjoyed most.

All of this would have been impossible, of course, without the help of my wife, Peggy, if only for her tolerance while I immersed myself in the research and writing. But there was also the infectious joy she takes in L.A., which aided my efforts. For this, and for herself, she has my love.

BIBLIOGRAPHY

Ever since Father Juan Crespi came across the Indian village of Yang-na in 1769 and christened it "El Rio de Nuestra Senora la Reina de los Angeles de Porciuncula," and described it at length in his diaries, scores of travelers, journalists, and authors who followed have been compelled to write about L.A. As a result, there is a wealth of literature and studies on L.A., some good, some bad, some perceptive, some obtuse.

Particularly useful to me in shaping my views were *Southern California: An Island on the Land*, by Carey McWilliams; *Los Angeles: The Architecture of Four Ecologies*, by Reyner Banham; *The Architecture of Los Angeles*, by Paul Gleye; and *Inventing the Dream*, by Kevin Starr. Each was informative as well as engaging, a rare combination for most histories.

They, and others I cite in my narrative, are listed below. Also listed are other readings that, while not quoted, I found pertinent:

Adamic, Louis. *Laughing in the Jungle*. 1932. Ayer Company, 1969.

Alleman, Richard. *The Movie Lover's Guide to Hollywood*. Harper, 1985.

Babitz, Eve. *Slow Days, Fast Company*. Pocket Books, 1978.

Banham, Reyner. *Los Angeles: The Architecture of Four Ecologies*. Penguin, 1973.

Bartlett, Dana. *The Better City*. Neuner Company Press, 1907.

Brodsly, David. *L.A. Freeway: An Appreciative Essay*. University of California Press, 1981.

Caughey, John and La Ree. *Los Angeles: Biography of a City*. University of California Press, 1977.

Chandler, Raymond. *The Big Sleep*. 1939. Vintage, 1977.

———. *Farewell My Lovely*. 1940. Vintage, 1976.

———. *The Little Sister*. 1949. Ballantine, 1971.

———. *The Long Goodbye*. 1954. Ballantine, 1977.

Chase, John, with John Beach. "The Stucco Box." An essay in *Home Sweet Home*, edited by Charles Moore. Rizzoli, 1984.

Clark, David. *Los Angeles: A City Apart*. Windsor, 1981.

———. *L.A. on Foot*. Camaro, 1976.

Cook, Peter. "Enigmatic Flower," *Progressive Architecture*, June, 1984.

Crouch, Winston W., and Beatrice Dinerman. *Southern California Metropolis*. University of California Press, 1963.

Crow, Charles, ed. *Itinerary: Criticism; Essays on California Writers*. Bowling Green University Press, 1978.

Devereaux, George. "In the Land of the Bungalow." Lyrics quoted in *The California Bungalow*, by Robert Winter. Hennessey & Ingalls, 1980.

Didion, Joan. *Play It As It Lays*. Bantam, 1971.

Dunne, John Gregory. *True Confessions*. Dutton, 1977.

Fine, David, ed. *Los Angeles in Fiction*. University of New Mexico Press, 1984.

Fogelson, Robert M. *The Fragmented Metropolis: Los Angeles, 1850 – 1930.* Harvard University Press, 1967.

Gebhard, David, and Harriette Von Breton. *L.A. in the Thirties, 1931 – 1941*. Peregrine Smith, 1972.

———. *Schindler*. Viking, 1972.

222

—————, and Robert Winter. *A Guide to Architecture in Los Angeles and Southern California*. Peregrine Smith, 1977.

—————, ed. *Myron Hunt, 1868 – 1952, The Search for a Regional Architecture*. Hennessey & Ingalls, 1984.

Gill, Brendan. *The Dream Come True*. Lippincott & Crowell, 1980.

Giovannini, Joseph. *Real Estate As Art: New Architecture in Venice*. Sewell Archives, 1984.

Girouard, Mark. *Cities & People*. Yale University Press, 1985.

Gleye, Paul. *The Architecture of Los Angeles*. Rosebud Books, 1981.

Grimond, John. *Los Angeles Comes of Age*. The Economist, 1982.

Halpren, John. *Los Angeles: Improbable City*. Dutton, 1979.

Heimann, Jim, and Rip Georges. *California Crazy*. Chronicle, 1980.

Henstell, Bruce. *Sunshine and Wealth: Los Angeles in the Twenties and Thirties*. Chronicle, 1985.

Hess, Alan. *Googie*. Chronicle, 1986.

Hines, Thomas. *Richard Neutra and the Search for Modern Architecture*. Oxford University Press, 1982.

Huxley, Aldous. *After Many a Summer Dies the Swan*. 1939. Harper, 1976.

Jenks, Charles. *Daydream Houses of Los Angeles*. Rizzoli, 1978.

—————. *Bizarre Architecture*. Rizzoli, 1979.

Kaplan, Samuel. *The Dream Deferred*. Vintage, 1976.

Lambert, Gavin. *The Slide Area*. Viking, 1959.

Landau, Robert, and John Pashdag. *Outrageous L.A.* Chronicle, 1984.

Lillard, Richard G. "Problems in Promise in Tomorrowland." *California History* 60 California Historical Society, 1981.

—————. *Eden in Jeopardy: The Southern California Experience*. Knopf, 1966.

Lockwood, Charles. *Dream Palaces*. Viking, 1981.

—————. *The Guide to Hollywood and Beverly Hills*. Crown, 1984.

Makinson, Randell L. *Greene & Greene: Architecture as Fine Art*. Peregrine Smith, 1977.

—————. *Greene & Greene: Furniture and Related Designs*. Peregrine Smith, 1978.

McCoy, Esther. *Five California Architects*. Praeger, 1960.

—————. *The Second Generation*. Peregrine Smith, 1984.

—————. *Case Study Houses, 1945 – 1962*. 2d ed. Hennessey & Ingalls, 1977.

—————. *Vienna to Los Angeles: Two Journeys*. A and A Press, 1979.

McWilliams, Carey. *Southern California: An Island on the Land*. 1946. Peregrine Smith, 1973.

Meyer, Larry L., ed. "Los Angeles, 1781 – 1981." *California History* 60 California Historical Society, 1981.

Moore, Charles, with Kathryn Smith, Peter Becker, eds. *Home Sweet Home*. Rizzoli, 1984.

—————, and Gerald Allen. *Dimensions: Space, Shape and Scale in Architecture*. Architectural Record Books, 1976.

—————, and Peter Becker, Regula Campbell. *The City Observed: Los Angeles*. Vintage, 1984.

Nadeau, Remi. *Los Angeles from Mission to Modern City*. Longmans, Green, 1960.

Nelson, Howard J. *The Los Angeles Metropolis*. Kendall/Hunt, 1983.

Newmark, Harris. *Sixty Years in Southern California*. 1916. Dawson's Book Shop, 1984.

Pereira, William, quoted in "Vistas for the Future," *Time*, September 6, 1963, and from personal interview, September 1981.

Pierson, Robert John. *The Beach Towns: A Walker's Guide*. Chronicle, 1985.

Polyzoides, Stefanos, and Roger Sherwood, James Tice. *Courtyard Housing in Los Angeles*. University of California Press, 1982.

Rand, Christopher. *Los Angeles, The Ultimate City*. Oxford University Press, 1967.

Robinson, W.W. "The Southern California Real Estate Boom of the Twenties," *Southern California Quarterly* 24, 1942; also in *Los Angeles: Biography of a City*, edited by John and LaRee Caughey, University of California Press, 1977.

———. *Los Angeles from the Days of the Pueblo*. California Historical Society, 1981.

Sanchez, Thomas. *Zoot-Suit Murders*. 1978. Pocket Books, 1980.

Stanton, Jeffrey. *Venice of America, 1905 – 1930*. ARS Publications, 1980.

Starr, Kevin. *Americans and the California Dream*. Oxford University Press, 1973.

———. *Inventing the Dream*. Oxford University Press, 1984.

Steiner, Rodney. *Los Angeles, The Centrifugal City*. Kendall/Hunt, 1981.

Walker, Derek, ed. *Los Angeles*. Architectural Design/St. Martin's, 1981.

Walker, Franklin. *A Literary History of Southern California*. University of California Press, 1950.

Waugh, Evelyn. *The Loved One*. Little Brown, 1950.

Weaver, John D. *L.A. El Pueblo Grande*. Ward Ritchie Press, 1973.

———. "The Laboratory of Marvels." *California History* 60 California Historical Society, 1981.

West, Nathanael. *Miss Lonelyhearts*, and *The Day of the Locust*. New Directions, 1962.

Winter, Robert. *The California Bungalow*. Hennessey & Ingalls, 1980.

Wurman, Richard Saul. *Los Angeles-Access*. Access Press, 1985.

PHOTO CREDITS AND PERMISSIONS

Grateful acknowledgment is given for the following excerpts:

From *Southern California: An Island on the Land* by Carey McWilliams. Copyright 1946 by Peregrine Smith Publishers. Reprinted by permission of Gibbs M. Smith, Inc.

From *California History*, LX, No. 1 (Spring 1981), page 95.

From *A Place in the Sun* by Frank Fenton. Reprinted by permission of Random House, Inc.

From *Fray Juan Crespi, Missionary Explorer on the Pacific Coast, 1769–1774* by Herbert E. Bolton. Reprinted by permission of Random House, Inc.

From *Vienna to Los Angeles: Two Journeys* by Esther McCoy. Copyright © 1979 by Esther McCoy. Reprinted by permission of the author.

From *The Day of the Locust* by Nathanael West. Copyright 1939 by the Estate of Nathanael West, renewed © 1966 by Laura Perelman. Reprinted by permission of New Directions Publishing Corporation.

From *The Dream Come True: Great Houses of Los Angeles* by Brendan Gill. Copyright © 1980 by Brendan Gill. Reprinted by permission of Harper & Row Publishers, Inc.

Grateful acknowledgment is given for the photographs appearing on the following pages. Every effort has been made to trace the proper copyright holders of the photographs used herein. If there are any omissions we apologize and will be pleased to make any corrections in future printings.

Page 12, used by permission of the Academy of Motion Picture Arts and Sciences. Page 185 (*bottom*), by Max Aguilera-Hellweg. Used by permission of the Museum of Contemporary Art, Los Angeles. Page 184 (*bottom*), copyright © 1982 by Glen Allison. Used by permission of the photographer. Page 145 (*bottom*), used by permission of Armet & Davis, AIA, Architects. Page 193, courtesy of Atlantic Richfield Company. Pages 92–93, 120 (*top*), 192 (*left*), 194, 195 (*top*), 197 (*top*), 198, 207 (*top*), 207 (*bottom left*), 211, copyright © by Bruce Boehner. Used by permission of the photographer. Pages 32 and 33, used by permission of the Bancroft Library, University of California. Page 26, used by permission of the Hotel Bel-Air. Pages 80, 81, 82 (*bottom*), 84, 85 (*top*), 85 (*center*), 85 (*bottom*), 86 (*top*), 86 (*bottom*), used by permission of Bison Archives. Pages 114 and 115 used by permission of Bullocks Wilshire. Pages 17, 36, 37 (*top*), 38 (*bottom*), 40 (*bottom*), 41 (*bottom*), 47 (*top*), 47 (*center*), 47 (*bottom*), 52 (*top*), 54 (*top left*), 54 (*top right*), 54 (*bottom*), 61, 64, 65 (*top*), 68 (*bottom*), 72, 76–77, 82 (*top*), 207 (*bottom right*), used by permission of the California Historical Society/Ticor Title Insurance (Los Angeles) Collection of Historical Photographs. Pages 87, 145 (*top*), by Frank Cooper. Used by permission of Los Angeles Conservancy. Pages 188, 189 (*right*), by Annette Del Zoppo. Used by permission of the photographer. Pages 162–163 copyright © 1984 by John Gaylord, page 200 (*right*), copyright © 1986 by John Gaylord, page 200 (*left*), copyright © 1982 by John Gaylord. Used by permission of the photographer. Page 169, by Steve Heller, used by permission of the photographer and the Art Center College of Design. Pages 28–30, 37 (*bottom*), 38 (*top*), 40–41 (*top*), 46, 48

(*bottom*), 49, 50, 52 (*bottom*), 56 (*top*), 56 (*center*), 60, 62, 66–67, 68 (*top*), 71 (*top*), 71 (*bottom*), 78, 91 (*top left*), 91 (*bottom left*), 91 (*top right*), 91 (*center right*), 91 (*bottom right*), 94–95, 116 (*top*), 116 (*bottom*), 124, 205, used by permission of The Huntington Library, San Marino, California. Pages 65 (*bottom*), 142 (*top*), 142 (*bottom*), 183 (*top*), collection of Margaret Hall Kaplan. Page 164, copyright © 1984 by Richard J. Levy. Used by permission of the photographer and David Hyun on behalf of Japanese Village Plaza Ltd. Pages 74, 89, 117, 120, 190, 201, 206, used by permission of Los Angeles Conservancy. Pages 22, 150, 151, 165, 204 (*bottom*), copyright © by the Los Angeles Times. Used by permission of the publisher. Page 175, used by permission of Anthony J. Lumsden/DMJM. Page 192 (*right*), by Randall Mitchelson, courtesy of Ratkovitch & Bowers. Pages 176, 178, 179, copyright © by Ronald Moore. Used by permission of the photographer. Page 180, by Michael Moran. Courtesy of American Institute of Architects. Page 284 (*top*), by Michael Moran. Courtesy of Museum of Contemporary Art, Los Angeles. Pages 186–187, by Chris Morland. Used by permission of Los Angeles Community Redevelopment Agency. Page 188 (*left*), courtesy of Nakashima Tschoegl & Associates. Page 154, by Levon Parian. Used by permission of Kamnitzer & Cotton. Pages 217 (*top*), 217 (*bottom*), used by permission of Pasadena Heritage. Pages 42 (*top*), 42 (*bottom*), used by permission of Pasadena Historical Society. Pages 59, 177 (*right*), 188–189 (*top*), 202, by Marvin Rand. Used by permission of the photographer. Pages 218–219, by George Rose. Used by permission of the photographer. Pages 4–5, 20, 90, by Iris Schneider. Used by permission of the photographer. Page 181, by Herb Shoebridge. Used by permission of the California Museum of Science and Industry. Jacket, pages 2–3, 10–11, 14, 15 (*bottom*), 18, 24, 25, 27, 34, 35, 44, 48 (*top*), 58, 96, 98–99 (*top*), 98 (*bottom left*), 98 (*bottom right*), 99 (*bottom*), 100–101, 101 (*bottom right*), 102, 104–105, 106 (*top*), 106 (*bottom left*), 106 (*bottom right*), 107 (*top*), 108, 109, 110 (*top*), 110 (*bottom*), 111 (*top*), 111 (*bottom*), 112–113, 120 (*bottom*), 121, 126, 130 (*bottom*), 131, 132, 133, 134–135, 135 (*right*), 136 (*top*), 136 (*bottom*), 137, 138, 139, 140 (*top*), 140 (*bottom*), 141, 144 (*top*), 144 (*bottom left*), 144 (*bottom right*), 146–147, 147 (*right*), 148, 152, 156, 157, 158–159, 160–161, 166, 167, 168, 170–171, 172, 182 (*top*), 182 (*bottom*), 184 (*bottom*), 195 (*bottom*), 196 (*top*), 196 (*bottom*), 197 (*center*), 199 (*top*), 203, 204 (*top*), 204 (*center*), 209 (*bottom*), 212, 213, 214, 216, by Julius Shulman. Used by permission of the photographer. Pages 122, 208, 209 (*top*), 215 (*center*), 215 (*bottom*), by Carlos von Frankenberg. Used by permission of Julius Shulman Associates. Pages 210, 215 (*top*), used by permission of Geraint O. Smith. Page 88, Title Insurance and Trust Company (Los Angeles) Collection of Historical Photographs. Used by permission of Los Angeles Conservancy. Page 107 (*bottom*), used by permission of the University Art Museum (Architectural Drawing Collection), University of California at Santa Barbara. Page 199, used by permission of Venice Action Committee. Pages 174, 175, by Anthony P. Verebes. Used by permission of Anthony Lumsden. Pages 118–119, 149, 185 (*top*), used by permission of Welton Becket Associates. Pages 128–129, 130 (*top*), 143, used by permission of The Whittington Collection, California State University, Long Beach. Page 177 (*left*), by Toshi Yoshimi. Used by permission of Johannes Van Tilburg & Partners.